Advance Praise for *Integrated Enterprise Excellence, Volume I—The Basics*

"This is a wonderful and insightful reference book."
—René Kapik, ASQ Certified BB; MBB
Senior Continuous Improvement Engineer, Precision Fabrics Group, Inc.

"[Forrest] takes us to the next level of skill development using Six Sigma to improve customer service and bottom line growth."
—Janet L Hammill, Business Process Excellence Lead, MBB, Rohm and Haas Company

"A text that will help all levels and players in a business organization better understand the principles of Lean Six Sigma."
—Keith Moe, Retired Executive VP, 3M

"Other books are light years behind Forrest's 4-book suite, which not only provides senior management with Lean Sigma performance Scorecards, but also a how-to roadmap for Enron-effect avoidance."
—Frank Shines, Black Belt, TDLeanSigma, Director, Tech Data Corporation
Author, *The New Science of Success*

"If you are a leader of an organization and you are a golfer, then Forrest Breyfogle has written an excellent novel to introduce you to the basic principles of Lean and Six Sigma. This [book] is an entertaining and effective story to help you comprehend and deploy these principles for the benefit of your strategic goals."
—Andy Paquet - Instructor, Central Michigan University College of Business, Certified Master Black Belt, Retired MBB & Scientist, The Dow Chemical Company

"Forrest Breyfogle has captured his IEE model in three volumes, which are a comprehensive work on how to deploy Six Sigma. Subjects range from the executive deployment of Lean Six Sigma as a business process, to Six Sigma project management, where numerous examples are used to illustrate

powerful Lean Six Sigma tools. Many of Forrest's examples and topics challenge traditional approaches. I routinely refer to the volumes to help solve many of my work related challenges."
—Brian Zievis, Global Technical Manager, BOC Edwards

Integrated Enterprise Excellence
Volume I—The Basics

Integrated Enterprise Excellence Volume I—The Basics

Golfing Buddies Go Beyond Lean Six Sigma and the Balanced Scorecard

Forrest W. Breyfogle III
Founder and CEO
Smarter Solutions, Inc.

Forrest@SmarterSolutions.com
www.SmarterSolutions.com
Austin, Texas

BridgewayBooks

Integrated Enterprise Excellence, Volume I—The Basics: Golfing Buddies Go Beyond Lean Six Sigma and the Balanced Scorecard

Published by Bridgeway Books in cooperation with Citius Publishing, Inc, Austin, TX

Excerpts from Harvey Penick's *Little Red Book* reprinted with the permission of Simon & Schuster Adult Publishing Group from Harvey Penick's *Little Red Book* by Harvey Penick with Bud Shrake. Copyright © 1992 by Harvey Penick and Bud Shrake, and Helen Penick

For more information about our books, please write to us, call 512.478.2028, or visit our website at www.bridgewaybooks.net.

Library of Congress Control Number: 2007936771

ISBN-13: 978-1-934454-12-1
ISBN-10: 1-934454-12-5

Cover concept design by Priyanka Kodikal.

10 9 8 7 6 5 4 3 2 1

To my beloved wife, Becki, who has made so many sacrifices in support of my work.

Contents

Foreword

Since the time of cave paintings, stories have helped people express their ideas. A story has the unique ability to engage, inform, persuade and motivate; all at the same time. This is true in business no less than in any other human endeavor. This was demonstrated with a highly successful business book, *The Goal*, in which Eliyahu M. Goldratt introduced to business the theory of constraints in the form of a novel.

Forrest Breyfogle has rivaled Mr. Goldratt with a novel about performance improvement lessons discovered, by four buddies, through the game of golf. Utilizing Mr. Goldratt's innovative approach, Breyfogle presents his Integrated Enterprise Excellence (IEE) system; integrating business scorecards, strategies, and process improvement. Through Volumes 2 and 3 of the series, the reader learns the how-to's of implementation in sophisticated detail.

The reader will be compelled by the plot's development and identify with the characters by vicariously sharing in their triumphs and disappointments. They will learn, along with the story's character, the basics of IEE's principles and how, as with golf, they can be applied to business management.

Understanding IEE is essential in today's hyper-competitive environment. The system meets complex challenges by helping businesses establish, what the author refers to as, the 'Three Rs' of business: 'Every employee doing the Right things Right... at the Right time.'

The running subtext of the novel explains how to apply appropriate corrections and achieve success by applying the proven guidance of legend Harvey Penick's "Little Red Book."

In the novel, friends seek to improve their golf game; as well as their businesses. Over a period of time, each friend discovers a way to apply IEE principles to resolve a specific business problem. Each example demonstrates the versatility of IEE, which encourages creative application of commonly available, proven management tools structured with discipline. Through the experience, the friends share in one another's enthusiasm and disappointments; victories and failures. Ultimately, they realize that success is achieved through a comprehensive and integrated approach to identifying goals and managing results.

In this; his latest publication, Breyfogle urges business leaders and associates to realize that Six Sigma and Lean concepts and practices, integrated under the umbrella of IEE, can achieve greater, sustainable performance and bottom-line results than they have attained before. The book emphasizes that these concepts can be utilized to identify the most significant improvement opportunities; while supplying practitioners with vital tools for exacting measurable, bottom-line improvement.

An essential handbook for every manager leading Six Sigma or Lean Six Sigma teams; it is also geared for managers who are uncertain as to their need for these initiatives. For all readers, the section which includes 'Why commonly used dashboards are misguided' and 'Alternative methods that actually improve performance' should prove particularly enlightening. It shows how creative managers can combine innovative and proven techniques to achieve results that are well beyond the norm!

IEE's structure compounds innovation, with analytics in the balance, that is correct for an organization's culture and strategy. An execution roadmap integrates Lean and Six Sigma activities; regardless of whether the industry is manufacturing or transactional. All process improvement tools are integrated as well. The structure measures only what matters. Every metric has an owner and priorities are determined by the familiar DMAIC (Define, Measure, Analyze, Improve, Control) sequence; up and down the value chain.

The process makes significant contributions to the organization in many ways. Gone are the times when projects are selected in isolation from one another. Also gone, are improvements made at the periphery of an organization, instead of in critical success paths. This is when, after harvesting low hanging fruit projects, improvement efforts typically stall.

Through IEE, work is also standardized, with certainty, to reduce variability, improve quality and results for the needs of internal and external customers alike. The flow of materials and information becomes seamless. The process ensures a reduced possibility of an incorrect shift of resources from one part of an organization to another. Employee avoidance of responsibilities and the use of metrics to hide shortfalls are also reduced when IEE measurements are in place.

Gains from IEE are perpetual. Once adopted and firmly established, IEE stays in place regardless of management continuity, competitive changes or economic conditions.

The management process perfected by Smarter Solutions was developed, utilizing modern enterprise management theory and practice, by establishing a process for both operational and corporate levels. The result facilitates new knowledge and methods in sustaining, innovating and growing businesses against demanding conditions.

The IEE model launches deployment with a powerful, week-long workout (described in Volume 2). Representatives with our company began the process in this way. On Monday, of the week-long session at our facility, our executive team was introduced to IEE. On Tuesday through Thursday, the Smarter Solutions team worked with our black belt trainees to build an Enterprise-DMAIC framework. By Friday, the executive team viewed a roughed-out structure for implementing IEE at our facility; one that our black belt trainees to immediately begin refining. We value this deployment model, which begins with implementation at one facility and later replicates the IEE system at other facilities. The risks of a deployment failure are reduced while the potential rewards significant.

Breyfogle has authored an innovative tool which, when implemented, offers management systems that effectively combine the attainment of business goals with well-documented management tools. The development of Integrated Enterprise Excellence creates a new vista of excellence in an increasingly challenging business environment. It offers impactful techniques; embracing a wide range of management disciplines.

This book is loaded with examples of how analytical and decision support techniques can be merged to create enterprise growth and progress. It includes methods like Lean, Six Sigma and Design of Experiments. Innovative thinking is embraced with IEE, as it is on the golf course. Traditional measurements and controls are challenged with alternative methods, using real world examples, to eliminate hazards and provide clear paths for successful scores. Through IEE, Forrest Breyfogle offers a vehicle to produce leaders who are teachers and teachers who are leaders. This book represents a valuable tool for both.

J. Scott Dickman, CEO
Oracle Packaging Company

Preface

Written as a novel, Volume 1 of this three-volume series helps managers, leaders, practitioners, and others *understand the basics* of the Integrated Enterprise Excellence (IEE) system that resolves the following frequently encountered problems:

- Business goals are not being met
- Scorecards often lead to the wrong activities
- Day-to-day firefighting of problems that don't seem to go away
- Business strategies that are very generic and/or difficult to translate to organizational work environments
- Lean events and other improvement projects consume a lot of resource but often do not have much, if any, quantifiable benefit to the business as a whole
- Lean Six Sigma:
  - Existing deployment that has projects, which are either not timely completed or reporting large financial claims that often cannot be translated into true benefits for the business as a whole
  - Existing deployment that has stalled out and needs rejuvenation
  - New deployment desires to create a system where improvement and design projects are in true alignment to business needs, and where projects are executed using an effective roadmap that truly integrates Six Sigma with Lean tools

This volume follows four successful friends who met in graduate school while pursuing their MBAs. Now they meet for a monthly golf outing to continue their friendship, discuss their careers, and compete in a friendly golf game for the price of dinner. The challenges they face in business and in their personal lives are all too familiar. Golf provides an intriguing metaphor for the game of life, with its complexities and challenges, changing conditions, chances for creativity, penalties, and rewards. Moreover, golf is the game most often associated with business. As Hank, Jorge, Wayne, and Zack share their experiences and pursuit of improvement in this Volume 1, they discover powerful new insights that help them see how they can improve their games, both in business and in golf.

SERIES DESCRIPTION: AN INTEGRATED SET OF REFERENCES

This is the first volume of a three-volume series that document the Integrated Enterprise Excellence (IEE) system—a set of management techniques that when effectively implemented improve an organization's measurement and improvement system so that there is an increase in predictable and sustainable bottom-line benefits. The IEE system embeds a set of best practices derived from the strengths of past systems—applying structured metrics and a nononsense roadmap to initiate process improvement and achieve substantial benefits. IEE takes Lean Six Sigma and the balanced scorecard to the next level in the pursuit of enterprise excellence.

The book, The Integrated Enterprise Excellence System: An Enhanced, Unified Approach to Balanced Scorecards, Strategic Planning, and Business Improvement, (Breyfogle 2008d) introduced new perspectives on what to measure and report; when and how to report it; how to interpret the results; and how to use the results to establish goals, prioritize work efforts and continuously enhance organizational focus and success.

In this three-volume series, *Integrated Enterprise Excellence: Beyond Lean Six Sigma and the Balanced Scorecard* (Breyfogle 2008 a, b, c), there is both further elaboration on the shortcomings of traditional systems and the details of an IEE implementation.

A content summary of this volume series is:

- *Integrated Enterprise Excellence Volume I—The Basics: Golfing Buddies Go Beyond Lean Six Sigma and the Balanced Scorecard*—An IEE onset story about four friends who share their experiences while playing golf. They see how they can improve their games in both business and golf using this system that goes beyond Lean Six Sigma and the balanced scorecard. The story compares IEE to other improvement systems (Breyfogle 2008a).

- *Integrated Enterprise Excellence Volume II—Business Deployment: A Leaders' Guide for Going Beyond Lean Six Sigma and the Balanced Scorecard*—Discusses problems encountered with traditional scorecard, business management, and enterprise improvement systems. Describes how IEE helps organizations overcome these issues utilizing an enterprise process define-measure-analyze-improve-control (E-DMAIC) system. Volume II systematically walks through the execution of this E-DMAIC system (Breyfogle 2008b).
- *Integrated Enterprise Excellence Volume III—Improvement Project Execution: A Management and Black Belt Guide for Going Beyond Lean Six Sigma and the Balanced Scorecard*—Describes IEE benefits and its measurement techniques. Provides a detailed step-by-step project define-measure-analyze-improve-control (P-DMAIC) roadmap, which has a true integration of Six Sigma and Lean tools (Breyfogle 2008c).

Volumes of this series build upon each other so that readers develop an appreciation and understanding of IEE and the benefits of its implementation. Each volume and this book are also written to stand alone. Because of this, several concepts and examples are described in more than one book or volume. I also felt it was important to repeat key concepts in multiple publications because each book or volume is more than a discussion of tools and examples – that is, each book and volume presents IEE so that the reader gains insight into the interconnection of the concepts and how they can benefit from the techniques.

OVERVIEW

Businesses that have adopted the Lean Six Sigma methodology have a built-in foundation for implementing this enhanced system. Others will learn how to establish the foundation for this system. For both groups, this series describes an enterprise process roadmap and a project execution roadmap, together with all the tools needed for achieving enterprise excellence.

This series of three volumes describes how to orchestrate activities, which can provide the highest yields at points where these efforts will have the greatest bottom-line impact. Effective orchestration ensures that activities will occur at the most opportune times throughout the entire organization.

Simply put, the described system helps an organization move toward the three Rs of business: everyone doing the Right things and doing them Right at the Right time throughout the organization. Rather than seeking out product or service flaws, this system determines whether the process itself is flawed. Rather than force projects where benefits could be questionable, designs and improvements are made that impact the overall systems for doing business. This system elevates every business unit to a new, more productive business way of life®.

The ultimate goal for an enterprise management system is to achieve maximum, measurable, predictable, and sustainable bottom-line results for the entire corporation. The volumes in this series describe an Integrated Enterprise Excellence (IEE) business management system, which presents the structure and tools you can use to accomplish these objectives. This IEE methodology provides a power-enhancing performance measurement scorecard/dashboard system that serves as an enterprise-wide route to increase corporate profitability continually.

This series describes how IEE takes Lean Six Sigma and the balanced scorecard to the next level. This system helps organizations overcome some difficulties encountered with previous systems. In IEE, a value chain performance measurement system provides organizations with a no-nonsense metric system that leads to the orchestration of day-to-day value-added activities so that there is true business-needs alignment. Improvement or design projects are created whenever business or operational metrics need betterment. This is in contrast to the search, selection, and creation of Six Sigma/Lean projects that often are not in true alignment with business goals. Organizations can gain a competitive advantage when this system becomes a business way of life.

This volume and other volumes of this series describe the IEE system, which addresses the following example needs:

- Executives want a structured system that can assist them with meeting their financial goals.
- An organizational executive or a change manager is looking for an enterprise management structure that will coordinate, track, enhance, control, and help predict corporate results.

- Leadership wants to become more of a data-driven/data-decision based company so that the right questions are asked before decisions are made.
- Executives want a system that helps them create a strategy that is more specifically targeted so that everyone has consistent focus toward meeting the organizational goals that they would like to achieve.
- Company leadership wants to reduce the amount of waste that they routinely experience when fighting the problems of the day, which never seem to go away.
- Management wants a no-nonsense measurement and improvement system.
- Leadership wants a streamlined enhancement to their Sarbanes-Oxley (SOX) system so that the company benefits more from its implementation with less effort.
- Lean Six Sigma deployment leaders want to integrate Lean and Six Sigma concepts and tools so that they are using the right tool at the right time.
- Management wants to improve its performance measurement and improvement systems.
- Managers and practitioners want an easy-to-follow roadmap that addresses not only project execution but also enterprise issues as well.
- Organization leaders want a system that can help them orchestrate people's activities so that everyone is doing the right things and doing them right at the right time.
- Lean Six Sigma deployment leaders want a system that consistently leads to projects that are most beneficial to the overall enterprise.

CEOs' benefits from this series include:

- CEOs want to avoid the problem: "Chiefs (CEOs) are being pushed out the door as directors abandon their laissez-faire approach to governance following the prosecutions at Enron Corp., WorldCom Inc., and other companies." (Kelly 2006)
- CEOs want to create a legacy system of organizational efficiency and effectiveness, which outlives their tenure as company heads.
- CEOs want to create more customers and cash.

When explaining the concepts to others, readers can reference volumes or portions of volumes at the other person's level of

Table 0.1: Where to start?

Where to start?		
Role	*I want to:*	*Source*
Executives, Champions, Managers, MBBs, BBs, GBs, and YBs	Assess the benefits of an IEE measurement and improvement system over other systems (novel format).	Volume 1
Executives, Champions, Managers, and MBBs	Understand the benefits of IEE when compared to other business systems and utilize a roadmap for IEE implemention at the enterprise level.	Volume 2
MBBs, BBs, GBs, and other practitioners	Execute effective process improvement projects, benefit from the project execution roadmap, and effectively utilize tools at both the project and enterprise level.	Volume 3

See Glossary for descriptions.

MBB = Master black belt   BB = Black belt   GB = Green belt   YB = Yellow belt

E-DMAIC (Roadmap): An IEE enterprise define-measure-analyze-improve-control roadmap, which contains among other things a value chain measurement and analysis system where metric improvement needs can pull for project creation.

P-DMAIC (Roadmap): An IEE project define-measure-analyze-improve-control roadmap for improvement project execution, which contains a true integration of Six Sigma and Lean tools.

understanding or need. Series volumes make reference to other volumes or *Implementing Six Sigma* (Breyfogle 2003) for an expansion of topic(s) or a differing perspective. These volumes are written to stand alone; however, there are some volume overlaps in the building of this IEE methodology series progression.

Table 0.1 describes how the volumes of this series can address differing readers' needs and interests. Note, the syntax for figure or table references in this volume series is that the first number is the chapter number. A zero was the first number in this table reference since the table is in the preface.

NOMENCLATURE AND SERVICE MARKS

The glossary and list of acronyms and symbols near the back of this volume are a useful reference for the understanding of unfamiliar statistical terms or acronyms/symbols. Book and publication references are also located near the back of this volume and will be referenced using the syntax (Author Name, Publication Date).

To maximize the clarification of illustrations that span several years, some examples include specific month-year entries. I did this at the risk of making the book appear to be dated in the years to come. Hopefully the reader will understand my reasoning for making this selection and this decision will not deter the reader from benefiting from the book's concepts for many years to come.

Integrated Enterprise Excellence, IEE, Satellite-level, 30,000-foot-level, and 50-foot-level are registered service marks of Smarter Solutions, Inc. In implementing the programs or methods identified in this text, you are authorized to refer to these marks in a manner that is consistent with the standards set forth herein by Smarter Solutions, Inc., but any and all use of the marks shall inure to the sole benefit of Smarter Solutions, Inc. Business way of Life and Smarter Solutions are registered service marks of Smarter Solutions, Inc.

ACKNOWLEDGMENTS

This volume is a derivative work of *Wisdom on the Green: Smarter Six Sigma Business Solutions* (Breyfogle, Enck, Flories, Pearson, et al. 2001).

Also I want to thank others who have helped with the creation of this volume. Lynn Cheshire helped through her editing and layout improvement suggestions. Fred Bothwell provided great manuscript and marketing inputs, along with superb publishing and printing coordination. Thanks also need to go to those who gave other helpful improvement suggestions or helped in some other way in the overall process: Bob Ashenbrenner, Becki Breyfogle, Bob Cheshire, Rick Haynes, Bob Jones, Mallary Musgrove, and George Nicholas.

Statistical analyses were conducted using Minitab. Flowcharts were created using Igrafx.

WORKSHOP MATERIAL AND ITS AVAILABILITY

We at Smarter Solutions, Inc. take pride in creating an excellent learning environment for the wise application of tools that will improve organizational business systems. Our IEE approach and workshop handout materials are continually being enhanced and expanded. Our training includes executive, champion, black belt, green belt, yellow belt, master black belt, Lean, and Design for Six Sigma (DFSS)/Design for Integrated Enterprise Excellence (DFIEE) courses. Workshops follow the E-DMAIC and P-DMAIC roadmaps, and often contain roadmap drilldowns not included in published books. Many who have already been trained as a black belt or master black belt have found our graduate workshop to be an excellent resource for their continuing education. This one-week graduate workshop walks through the IEE roadmaps, describing the unique measurements and tool applications, with benefits.

Licensing inquiries for training material can be directed through www.smartersolutions.com. Articles, newsletters, and the latest information on how Smarter Solutions, Inc. is working with various organizations and universities are also described at this website.

ABOUT SMARTER SOLUTIONS, INC, CONTACTING THE AUTHOR

Your comments and improvement suggestions for this book are greatly appreciated. For more information about business measurements and improvement strategies, sign up for our newsletter or e-mail us for a free initial business consultation.

FORREST W. BREYFOGLE III
Smarter Solutions, Inc.
11044 Research Blvd., Suite B-400
Austin, TX 78759, USA
Forrest@SmarterSolutions.com
www.smartersolutions.com
512-918-0280

1

The Starting Point

The Waggle

The waggle is ... a small practice swing and a way to ease tension....

... Bobby Jones said if you saw him waggle more than twice, he probably hit a bad shot.

Harvey Penick's Little Red Book (Penick with Shrake 1992)

March

Hank arrived early at the golf course and was hitting some balls to loosen up. The sky was crystal blue, and the wind was still. The weather was perfect for eighteen holes of golf, but Hank was having a hard time getting his mind off work.

As vice president of operations at Hi-Tech Computers, his background in electrical engineering and an MBA had helped make him a fast tracker. Hi-Tech was an aggressive, successful computer component manufacturer with plants in the southwestern United States and Mexico. Recently, however, it had been facing new competition and pressures from its biggest customers to comply with growing regulations, improve delivery times, become more flexible, and lower prices. Of course, they all wanted perfect products as well. Things were really heating up. Hank again tried to concentrate on golf.

Hank was tall and strong at 46 years old. He looked more like the former linebacker he had been in college than a PGA pro. He loved golf, but all attempts to improve on his 12 handicap seemed to fall victim to a few big numbers each round. If he could just eliminate those big mistakes, especially the penalty strokes for out-of-bounds and unplayable lies, he was sure he could achieve his goal of consistently breaking 80. After all, he thought, he could hit the ball a long way and often made great shots. He had a hole in one and a flock of eagles on his resume, but he could also hit it into trouble on the very next shot. If he could just eliminate the double bogeys (and worse), he would be happy with his game. Hank forced a resigned smile as he promised to practice more and to try harder this year. If work would ease up just a little, he could blitz this game. Hank loved to "grip it and rip it," the exact opposite of his regular playing partner, Jorge, who thought his way around the golf course as well as in the boardroom at Harris Hospital.

Hank thought for a moment about the possible root cause of his big numbers. Sometimes he hooked the ball, sometimes he sliced it, but usually he hit it pretty well. Once in a while it was dead-solid-perfect. He was proud of his ability to scramble, to recover from trouble, both on the course and when fighting fires at work. He just wished for fewer of those big mistakes that cost him extra time, constant reorganizations at work, and penalty strokes on the golf course. Yes, the increasing pressure from Hi-Tech's customers, shareholders, and regulators was eating into his golf practice time. Recently, more "snowmen," those nasty eights, were showing up on his scorecard than he cared to admit.

He was still engrossed in his thoughts when he saw his old college buddies, Jorge, Wayne, and Zack, walking toward the practice green. Their tee time was still twenty minutes away, so they caught up on family news as they practiced. Zack, always the serious one, was even able to slide in some business discussions about the latest investment model his company was developing that would produce a high rate of return with minimized risk. Meanwhile, he rolled in another long practice putt. Jorge was hitting a few of his magic chip shots from the fringe, while Wayne stretched and warmed up his smooth, rhythmic swing with his 7 iron.

***

As they approached the first tee, they agreed to their usual pairings: Hank and Jorge teamed against Wayne and Zack in a game of two-man best ball. The best individual score on each team determined who won the hole. The team that won the most holes could win the front nine, the back nine, and the total. Loss of two out of the three meant you picked up the tab for dinner.

Hank liked this game. He could play his own ball and keep his own score, make an occasional great shot, and still rely on steady old Jorge to carry him on a hole if he came up with one of those big numbers. The game had provided lots of camaraderie and good-natured competition over the years.

After winning the coin toss for honors, Hank stepped to the first tee and surveyed the 425-yard par 4. He didn't like this hole. It's not that he didn't like a challenge, but he preferred a simpler par 4 that gave him a chance to warm up a bit. This one was long and hard, demanding immediate execution from the very first swing. Closer inspection showed a Mexico-sized bunker guarding the next 75 yards along the inside of the dogleg about 150 yards out on the right side of the fairway. About 100 yards off the tee, a stream that today looked like the Rio Grande crossed the fairway. "Get those negative thoughts out of your head," Hank thought as he made his first swing. The muffled "click" told him immediately that he was in trouble. His new ball cleared the Rio Grande but disappeared weakly into the heart of Mexico.

Jorge was up next and hit a modest drive that ended up short but in play. Wayne stroked a beautiful 275-yard drive that successfully avoided the hazards that had befallen Hank, and then Zack hooked a drive into the light rough on the left.

Zack chided Jorge and Hank, "Looks like you guys will be picking up the tab tonight."

As they rode to their second shots, Jorge said, "Hank, you'd better get rid of that slice. I know it's been a while since our last game, but I don't want to lose to these guys again."

Hank bit his lip. He didn't have a slice problem. He just wasn't warmed up yet. He changed the subject. "My mind is still at work and not on this lousy game."

Hank stepped out of the cart and selected a 3 wood. It was a very difficult shot, but he was still 300 yards from the green, and on a long par 4 like this, Jorge would never be able to reach the green in two. Hank didn't want to start off too far behind in this match. His mind was churning and his swing was rushed as the mighty blow took mostly sand. The ball trickled only a few yards ahead, still in the trap. Hank's blood pressure rose as he hit the next two shots only a few yards each. Now he had really done it— blown the first hole on his way to another 8 or worse. There were still 40 yards of sand in front of him. Hank took a deep breath and tried to ignore the barbs flying from the other golf cart as he stepped out of the trap and exchanged his 3 wood for his trusty 5 iron. It wouldn't make it to the green, but it should get out of the trap and get him back in play. A mediocre swing advanced his ball out of the trap, just barely to the point where he had expected to find his original drive. "Four strokes wasted—I've done it again!" Hank fumed to himself.

As he climbed back into the cart, Jorge calmly said, "Why didn't you just chip the first one sideways back out into the fairway and save yourself a few strokes and a lot of grief?"

Hank fought back the urge to snap at his partner just long enough to realize the wisdom of his advice. He did that too often—threw good strokes after bad, compounding his original mistake by blindly charging straight ahead. How could someone who hit the ball no better than Jorge play him almost even? On most holes, Hank thought, he easily outplayed Jorge, but on a few holes each round Jorge would take a scrambling par or routine bogey while Hank exploded to a double bogey—or worse. When the final scores were tabulated, Jorge was almost always closer than you would expect and sometimes even beat Hank. Was there a smarter way to play this game? Was Jorge onto something?

As Hank tried to reason it out, he forgot about the comments coming from Wayne and Zack and began to settle down. When they reached his ball, he hit a smooth 6 iron on the green and two-putted for another dreaded 8. Fortunately, Jorge had scraped the ball along, getting close in three, hit another great chip shot within inches, and made the tap-in for bogey. Meanwhile, Wayne and Zack seemed distracted and made bogey as well.

"Hank, you'd better get your head in the game or we're gonna end up paying for dinner," Jorge prodded him.

"I told you that my mind is still at work," Hank responded.

"So what's the problem?" Jorge asked.

"I've been pressuring my managers to increase profit margins. They did it, alright, by shifting most of the connector assembly work to a couple of our plants in Mexico. The problem is that another manager discovered that our division had a component supplier inside Mexico with an even lower cost structure and decided to move half of the production to that plant."

Wayne who had been listening in on the conversation at the second tee empathized with Hank. "We are running into the same problems at Wonder-Chem. As with every company, there is always constant pressure from the Wall Street analysts to reduce costs and increase quarterly profits. Meanwhile, it seems like there's always another problem surfacing. For example, last month we had a major yield hit which held up delivery of our shampoo products to our northeast distributors due to a container defect. Our engineers were trying to cut costs with a new injection-molded container; however, the side wall of one of the corners was too thin, and 300,000 shampoo bottles leaked all over our warehouse floor when a cold front moved through."

> We are running into the same problems ... there is always constant pressure from the Wall Street analysts to reduce costs and increase quarterly profits. Meanwhile, it seems like there's always another problem surfacing.

Hank continued his story. "After transferring the equipment and operations, they found out that the third plant lacks the necessary quality and safety certifications, and it's not even set up to ship product to the United States! It's been a colossal screw-up!"

"Why didn't these issues surface when your management was researching lower-cost alternatives?" Jorge asked as he lined up to hit his driver on the second tee.

Watching Jorge, Hank remembered how long it always took his friend to prepare for his shot. "We could be out here all day," he thought, and decided to hold his reply until his partner finished. After all, there was a hefty dinner bill riding on the match.

Jorge waggled gently side to side, readjusting his stance, trying to avoid the inevitable. The driver had always been his weakest club and it pained him each time he reached for it. As expected, Jorge didn't break any driving records, but the ball went 175 yards straight down the fairway.

"You really need to get over your driver phobia if we're ever going to finish this round."

"Well, at least *I'm* on the fairway," Jorge responded with a slight smile.

"Whatever," Hank replied. "As I was saying, the management in Mexico assumed we knew about the certification and delivery issues. They were in the process of laying out a plan to ship product to a US plant using a certified freight forwarder that could ship between the US and Mexico. Can you imagine? They actually planned to use a middleman to ship product from Mexico to a plant in Oklahoma and then turn around and ship from Oklahoma to our customers!"

As he told the story, Hank began to burn with anger, "Our management team has spent the last two days developing a plan to meet current orders from our existing plants and move production back to the original two plants in Mexico. Instead of saving cost and labor, we've added millions to our expenses this year."

***

Once his story had been told, Hank began to refocus on his golf game. With his obligatory "snowman" out of the way, he actually played pretty well, recovering to shoot 85. Jorge struggled on the long holes but teamed well when Hank faltered to finish with 89. Wayne was solid as ever with his 76; just a few missed putts from shooting par. Zack used his wonderful putting stroke to stave off total disaster and finished with 96. Hank and Jorge lost the front side by one hole, but recovered to win the back nine holes by two and win the overall match. Later that evening, as Wayne and Zack split the dinner tab, Hank relived Jorge's beautiful 20-foot putt on the 18th green, which sealed their victory.

He was even able to tell a version of the old golf joke on himself. "Hey, Hank, how did you make 8 on the first hole? I just missed a 30-footer for my 7!"

Hank's friends wished him luck in solving his production problems. They all knew that Hank was really at his best when fighting fires. The interesting part would be hearing about his solution.

On the drive home, Hank thought about his good friends. There were many interesting similarities among them. They had played together for years, ever since they met in MBA classes at the university. They were all competitive, in golf and in business, and Hank thought it was no coincidence that they had all advanced to VP level in their respective companies. However, each had some unique traits.

Jorge was 47 and a senior vice president at Harris Hospital. Short and stocky, with a choppy golf swing due to an old soccer injury to his shoulder, he was good at keeping the ball down in the wind. He used his typical fade to great advantage as long as the shot did not require too much distance. His real trademark was his short game. Too often, it seemed Jorge was chipping on and one-putting while Hank was on in two and three-putting or worse. It wasn't so much that Jorge was a great putter; he wasn't as good as Zack, but he just didn't leave himself very many long or hard putts.

Wayne was 45, and a VP of Research and Development at Wonder-Chem. He had leveraged his BS in Chemistry and MBA to manage product development successfully for the last few years.

Wayne had the look of the former basketball player he had been, even though he was not especially tall. Fortunately, he had been a great shooter and a starting varsity guard in college. His conservative haircut, clothes, and bifocal glasses made him look more like an accountant than a scientist, but his precision golf swing was a thing of beauty. Ten years earlier, Hank had joked that he was going to invest for retirement by sponsoring Wayne on the Senior Tour when he reached fifty. Back then, Wayne had been almost a scratch golfer, but age seemed to be taking its toll. For several seasons Wayne had not putted as well, and his average had slipped into the upper 70s. That was good for the group competition; at least they didn't have to play 3 against 1 as they had in the beginning, but Hank wondered what had happened to Wayne's game.

For that matter, what had happened to his own game? He had slipped a few strokes as well, and now Jorge was beating him more often. He thought again about Jorge's "lesson" on the first hole today. It would bear more investigation.

Finally, there was Zack. Youngest of the group at 44, he looked even younger. He had the muscular build of a baseball player and the baseball swing to go with it. He was the most erratic of the group until he reached the green. Then the magic started. His eagle eye could read putts with the best of them and he spent lots of time practicing on the putting green. No one drained as many putts as Zack. Fortunately for Hank and Jorge, he was usually already out of the hole by then.

Yes, it was a good group. Good friends, good competition, good people. Unfortunately, as Hank pulled in the driveway, he remembered his problems at work and began to worry about what he would do next.

2

The Mexico Meeting

Do You Need Help?

If you play poorly one day, forget it.

If you play poorly the next time out, review your fundamentals of grip, stance, aim, and ball position. Most mistakes are made before the club is swung.

If you play poorly for a third time in a row, go see your professional.

Harvey Penick's Little Red Book (Penick with Shrake 1992)

One Week Later

Things were happening fast for Hank. One week after the golf outing he found himself on the way to Juarez, Mexico for a weeklong business trip. There would be many hours of meetings once he arrived, so he allowed himself a moment to relax and to think about the golf outing. Surprisingly, he had shot a pretty good score. It would have been very good if it hadn't been for that eight on the first hole. Maybe there was a lesson in Jorge's comments. Still, hindsight is usually 20/20. Once you have wasted three or four shots in a bunker, it's easy to say you should have played a safe shot out of the trap rather than risk a heroic shot with a 3 wood. Still, he could have made that shot. He'd done it before. Not that often, but he had! How do you know when to take a chance and when to play it smart? The odds of making the more difficult shot are lower, but the possible rewards are much higher. Did Jorge know the odds? Were the odds different for players with different skills? Should you always try to do what the pros would do, or should you sometimes take Jorge's advice and play it smart? Jorge was good at thinking his way around the course. He certainly did get more out of his limited physical skills than Hank. Did he just play more or was there really a solution that was smarter? Hank decided he should study this further, on the golf course, naturally.

How do you know when to take a chance and when to play it smart?

Suddenly thoughts of the Mexico meeting played through in his mind. Not only did he need to find a solution to the current production problems, but he also had to address the original business issues that led to the plant transfer in the first place. The plants needed to reduce costs and increase throughput to stay competitive in their market.

***

On Monday morning, Hank met with his new manufacturing director, Karen Johnson, and the production supervisors from the Juarez and Mexicali plants, Juan Rodriguez and Carlos Silva. Hank wanted to discuss how to salvage the current situation. Karen was a manufacturing engineer who had become a good manager. He liked Karen and trusted her judgment.

Just hours prior to the meeting, Hank had learned from an email that production at the Juarez plant had not been impacted by the move. Operations at their second plant in Mexicali had been transferred to a plant in Mexico City.

He also discovered that the original plant in Mexicali was not completely shutdown. During a five-hour marathon meeting, they decided that the best solution would be to transfer operations back to the Mexicali plant from Mexico City.

The complete waste of this undertaking was painful. Equipment transfer costs, lost sales, and setup costs were just the tip of the iceberg in terms of damage to the bottom-line.

The complete waste of this undertaking was painful. Equipment transfer costs, lost sales, and setup costs were just the tip of the iceberg in terms of damage to the bottom line. In preparation for its closing, they had also lost some of their best employees through layoffs at the Mexicali plant.

***

By Thursday morning the operations meeting was complete, and the business unit review was set to begin. The other key managers for the business unit flew in Wednesday night.

Because of a reorganization, the members were all new; however, the least-experienced member had been with the company for ten years so at least they weren't novices. The new members included John Jenkins, the supply chain manager; Ellen Simpson, the quality manager; and Andy Anderson, the marketing manager.

Hank opened the meeting with a clear plan in mind. "The purpose of this meeting is to define the problems of this business unit and develop a plan to solve them. I want to know all of the important problems you're facing. Anything not brought up today cannot be used as a crutch for future poor performance. Let's start with marketing."

Anderson stood and walked to the front of the room like a fifth grader who hadn't completed his homework. "Well," he stammered, trying to collect himself while plugging his laptop into the projector. "As you can see from this chart, we have gone from a 50 to 35% market share over the past year." To his surprise, Hank said nothing. Anderson was expecting some browbeating over the poor performance even though the deficiencies were due to his predecessors.

Anderson collected his thoughts and continued, "This reduction in market share is mainly due to three new competitors who have entered the market. This competition has turned the sub-assemblies we make into a commodity item. Customers are no longer willing to pay a premium for our brand name."

Hank responded in an even tone, "I would challenge some of your conclusions; however, the purpose of this meeting is to discover problems. Is there anything else?"

Anderson was thinking fast. He hadn't expected to get past the 15 point drop in market share, not with Hank's temper. Everyone was scared of Hank so they didn't always give him the complete story, but his reaction hadn't been so bad. Maybe he could tell him about the product delivery problem.

Here goes nothing, Anderson thought, as he advanced to the next chart and continued his presentation. "We're also losing customers because our delivery times are not meeting their needs."

> "We're also losing customers because our delivery times are not meeting their needs."

"Wait a minute," a shout came across the table. Rodriguez was on his feet in a flash. "That's not true! We have a near-perfect record of on-time delivery."

Anderson responded, "That's because our sales representatives tell customers our lead time is three weeks. Customers who need their product sooner don't order or they are forced to wait for three weeks and then don't reorder with us. Our competitors have a shorter lead time and…"

Rodriguez interrupted again, "But why didn't you say something!" Rodriguez was beside himself due to what he considered an unwarranted attack.

"We did!" Anderson responded forcefully. "If you had been listening…"

Hank interrupted them, "Okay, I see the problem. We'll work it out later. For now we're just defining the problems. Let's hear from supply chain next. John?"

Jenkins relaxed a bit as he stood. Maybe there would be no executions today after all. He spoke from his position at the conference table. "We have supplier and delivery problems. Our suppliers sometimes run out of inventory when we have a big order, and at other times we have weeks of inventory. Due to the complicated bidding process for our suppliers, the purchasing group head count has increased. Our delivery contractor can't seem to provide consistent delivery times and tends to lose orders on a fairly regular basis. Unfortunately, we are forced to use that particular contractor because purchasing negotiated a contract for the entire business unit."

"Is that it?" asked Hank. Jenkins nodded. Hank then asked Juan to summarize the key production issues in Juarez.

Juan stood and started through his list of problems. It seemed as if Hank had heard them all before: large finished-goods inventory, large amount of work in process, not enough storage space, changing schedules, missing parts, and quality problems.

> … heard them all before: large finished-goods inventory, large amount of work in process, not enough storage space, changing schedules, missing parts, and quality problems.

Finally he finished, and Hank asked, "Is that all?" Juan nodded.

"Great, now how are we going to fix these problems, people?" Hank asked with a steady, even stare.

No one said a word. Hank decided to wait for an answer.

After three minutes of silence that seemed like an hour, Carlos spoke, "When working for my previous employer, we used a different production method. It was called Lean, and it seemed to address many of the problems we discussed today."

Hank had heard of Lean and had even read some on the topic. After further discussions, Hank decided that he would look further into Lean techniques, but for now he was exhausted, and, he knew, so was everyone else in the meeting.

***

Hank was glad to be home. The trip to Mexico had been grueling, but worthwhile. Now, all he had to do was learn how to implement a Lean system, he thought with a smile. He decided to take Sunday off—after all, those problems would still be there Monday. Today, he would keep his other promise to himself and work on his golf. Driving to the practice range, he thought back over his last few rounds and tried to remember his worst holes. He was sure that if he improved on those two or three really bad holes each round, even if he just turned them into bogeys, he could save two or three strokes on each bad hole. The effort could easily make an improvement of five or six shots per round and get his average down close to 80. That would mean some rounds in the seventies. Look out, Wayne!

But how could he avoid those big meltdowns? If he followed Jorge's advice and always took the safe shot, he would give up any chance for the occasional great shot that got him a birdie or eagle. That seemed counter-productive, and not nearly as much fun. He paid for a large bucket of balls and decided that his driver set the stage for success or failure on most holes. A good long drive usually meant a chance at par or birdie, and it felt great when the others in the group "ooh'd" and "aah'd" over one of his really big hits. He smiled as he thought about last summer and the drive he had smoked 325 yards, followed by a beautiful 125-yard 8 iron, which fell for an eagle! They still talked about that one. On the other hand, he often hit a bad one like he did on the first hole at the last outing, got in trouble, and quickly degenerated to a double bogey or worse. Maybe he should just practice more with his driver. As he set the balls down on the range, he reached for the "big dog" and started to work. It was his favorite club. He'd work it out.

***

After a few phone calls on Monday, Hank was able to contact Lean and Mean Manufacturing Consultants (LMMC) and in short order was speaking with the president, Jason Sanders. Hank wanted to know more about Lean, and Jason was happy to give him a summary.

Jason started by talking about Lean production. "Lean focuses on the reduction of waste through the value stream. Even though the techniques originated in manufacturing, the ideas can be used for service or transactional processes. Even new product development can benefit from the methodology."

> Lean focuses on the reduction of waste through the value stream. Even though the techniques originated in manufacturing, the ideas can be used for service or transactional processes.

Jason continued, "Lean is a set of techniques used to reduce waste in business operations. The Toyota Production System or TPS, as it is sometimes called, is a good example of Lean implementation. Toyota has been developing its production philosophy and implementation tools since the 1950s."

Hank took the following notes on some basic principles of Lean principles and Lean tools:

- Don't overproduce: Make what the customer wants when he wants it. This holds true both for internal and external customers.
- Define customer value: Root out non-value-added activity.
- Focus on the entire value stream (supply chain): It does no good to reduce the time it takes to produce a product if the delivery system accounts for 80% of the product delivery time.
- Convert from batch processing to continuous flow whenever possible.
- Synchronize production between process steps.
- Develop ability to make your full product mix in any given day.
- Relentlessly pursue perfection.

Tools used to implement the Lean production philosophy include:

- The 5S procedures used to clean up and organize a work place (house keeping)
  1. Sort
  2. Straighten

    3.   Shine

    4.   Standardize Work

    5.   Sustain Improvements

- Store inventory close to where it will be used in production
- Reduce Setup Time

  This impacts the ability to make every part every day.

- Implement Production cells

  Production cells are pieces of equipment that are organized so that product can flow from one piece of equipment to the next during production. They work well when implemented with small batch sizes and pull production. This methodology also works well for non-manufacturing activities, such as development and transactional projects.

- Utilize Kanban Production Control

  Kanban production characterized by a small collection of inventory parts between each production workstation and no work done by a process step until the next process downstream uses some of the stored inventory.

What the Lean consultant said made sense to Hank. He would delegate the details of implementation to someone else in the organization while he oversaw the progress. He made a note to contact his manufacturing director, Karen Johnson, to have her meet with Jason to start putting an implementation plan together immediately. Hank smiled to himself as he hung up the phone. He liked working with Karen. She was smart and efficient. They would attack this problem head-on and solve it together.

He relaxed for a moment and thought about golf again. Maybe Lean could help there, too. Could it help eliminate those wasted second, third, or fourth shots? Hitting the bucket of balls on Sunday had certainly not helped much. Sure, there were some beautiful shots that turned heads on the range, but deep down Hank knew that at least ten percent of his drives were still unacceptable. That would have cost him strokes (rework?) on the course. Then he thought about Jorge's advice again and could not erase the feeling that there was something important in it.

3

Methods

Putting

One thing all great putters have in common, regardless of their style, is that the putting stroke is approximately the same length back and through.

... With short putts concentrate on the line.

With long putts concentrate on the distance.

Harvey Penick's Little Red Book (Penick with Shrake 1992)

April

Hank could hardly contain himself as he worked his way down the winding road from his house to the golf course. He was eager to tell his friends about the new program he implemented to solve the manufacturing problems in Mexico.

As he traveled the familiar route to the golf course, he randomly thought about his business. How many reorganizations had he done in the last three years? Was it four or five? Well, no matter, if the current leaders couldn't cut costs and increase throughput, he would just find someone who could.

To Hank, business was a form of combat. The object was to create a winning strategy, deploy your forces, and execute a plan, thereby destroying the opposition. In many ways it was just like football, Hank thought. After the fiasco last month, he had had to shake up his organization again. As he arrived at the golf course, his thoughts turned to the details of his current method of combat, the Lean Program.

Meanwhile, down on the practice green, Wayne watched the crowd gather to observe the spectacle that Zack and Jorge had created. They were betting on who could make the longest putt. They had started with five-foot putts and worked their way up to 15 feet. Jorge was completely focused, ignoring everyone at the moment. He knew every break on this practice green, and a lot was riding on this putt. He had just bet Zack leadership of the free world that he would sink this 25-footer.

Just as the putter started forward, Hank came down the hill yelling greetings to his friends. Jorge's concentration was remarkable as he stroked the putt and watched the ball gather speed down a slight incline, and then break three feet left to right just as he had predicted. Reaching the hole, the ball caught the far side of the cup, executed a complete 360-degree wrap around, and hung on the edge. A noticeable sigh rose from the assembled crowd. Then, just as everyone had given up on the shot, the blades of grass underneath the ball gave way, and the ball dropped into the cup.

Everyone around the green was cheering. Jorge was surprised at how much he enjoyed the accolades. As he smiled to himself, he thought, "Was it the putt or the fact that I've regained control over the free world?" Actually, it was the putt; neither he nor Zack had ever bothered to place an operational definition on what they meant by control of the free world. Jorge wasn't sure what he had won. In the end, he just enjoyed the competition.

"Great putt," Hank called out, "but save a few of those for our match, partner. Hey, you guys won't believe what's happened at work since last month!"

Jorge stopped him in mid-thought, "We're not going to start talking about work right away, are we? How 'bout talking about my beautiful putt for now?" he said with a laugh. Hank agreed impatiently to hold shoptalk until later.

***

By the fifth hole, Hank's earlier excitement began to resurface. While waiting for Zack to find his ball in the thick rough down the left side of the fairway, Hank again started to explain what had happened in the last month. "After the fiasco, I reorganized the manufacturing group and brought in a new director. Then I had her initiate a Lean program."

"From what I've learned about Lean, we should be able to respond more quickly to product-demand changes, reduce costs, and increase our throughput," Hank continued.

"I found my ball," Zack yelled. "Do you believe this rough? I almost needed a hedge trimmer just to get to my ball," he joked. At this point, the group wasn't paying any attention to Zack as talk had turned strictly business.

Hank continued, "All kinds of problems have brought our business to the brink of extinction. In order to develop a game plan for saving the business, we held a management review and decided to start a Lean program."

Wayne was getting interested. He had recently started discussions with his management team about what program they could initiate to help solve some of their company problems. Low yields, poor on-time delivery, raw material issues, and high costs were just a few of the chronic problems Wonder-Chem was facing. Wayne asked, "How will Lean reduce costs?"

Hank spent the better part of the ninth and tenth holes explaining what he had learned from Jason, his Lean consultant.

> Six Sigma is often considered a problem solving project-based quality improvement program.

Wayne explained that his executive team had heard a Lean Six Sigma presentation and decided to implement the program. He noted that Six Sigma and Lean Six Sigma are often considered a problem solving project-based quality improvement program. He pointed out that the Total Quality Management (TQM) initiative that Wonder-Chem had implemented some years ago had been abandoned. Their slogan had been:

> *Wonder-Chem is committed to being a company of the highest quality in every aspect of its business activity.*

There had been some good, isolated results from the TQM program, but not enough to capture upper management's attention or sustain the program.

In retrospect, Wayne felt the major problem with TQM was that the Quality Department had been chosen to implement it. Wonder-Chem's quality organization could be very hard-line and uncompromising with respect to how they viewed problems. They seemed to have no concern for overall business issues, with their total focus placed on quality. As a result, the Quality Department had a hard time getting operations managers to cooperate and let their people join the Quality Improvement Teams. Wayne remembered one meeting in particular during which the TQM program leaders demanded more top-management support and financial resources to address a long-range improvement, while ignoring the hard business reality that the funding they were requesting would severely impact production operations.

"This time I am going to do it differently with Lean Six Sigma," Wayne explained. "I am going to hire a Lean Six Sigma trained program leader to drive the program. He or she will be responsible for achieving financial goals through the completion of projects."

> I am going to hire a Lean Six Sigma trained program leader to drive the program. He or she will be responsible for achieving financial goals through the completion of projects.

"TQM really was a good initiative," Hank interjected. "In fact, we went through TQM training some years ago and got some good results here and there. I heard that Lean Six Sigma was an improvement over TQM in that practitioners worked on projects that had finance-validated savings."

Zack walked up complaining about his horrible shot. "This hole is going to ruin my round. This isn't my typical game."

"Not your typical game?" chided Wayne. "Every time we play, you run into several holes that kick your butt. Maybe you need a new driver, one you can keep in play," he said with a sly grin.

For an instant, Hank was distracted from the business discussion. Zack had lots of flaws that cost him strokes; what he needed was a new swing. He thought for a moment about his own game. Maybe one of the new over-sized titanium drivers would be just the cure for his bad hole or two each round.

Then Zack switched topics to offer his perspective on the business discussions. "One of our directors heard about a concept called the balanced scorecard, and has been very excited about the prospects, so I decided to look into the methodology."

"The balanced scorecard, what is that?" Hank responded.

"The balanced scorecard is a technique to track the business in the areas of financial, customer, and internal business processes, as well as in learning and growth. The organization's vision and strategy formulate these metrics. Each category is to have objectives, measures, targets, and initiatives," Zack answered.

"How do you know how well a metric is doing relative to its target?" Wayne interjected.

"The scorecard uses green, yellow, and red colors to describe the current performance level. Tables or graphs present the current metric status. If the color is green, the metric performance is satisfactory relative to achieving its target or plan. If the color is yellow, the current level of performance is marginal. If the color is red, the current level of performance is not satisfactory and corrective action should be undertaken."

Wayne interrupted, "That seems simple; however, I have concerns about creating metrics from strategies. I don't know about your company's strategies but ours often appears to be simply a bunch of words. In addition, these words could have multiple interpretations and can change significantly between years."

"Yes, I have had that same concern," Zack said. "Everyone was excited that this methodology could be a means to implement our strategic plan. From the metric color, we could now know when corrective action needed to be taken. However, I am not so confident in our current strategies. We could be having people react to things that are not real or important. Also, since our targets get set each year, it would seem that we could get a metric disconnect each year."

Wayne interjected, "I have never felt really good about the wording of our strategic plan statements. We typically assess and make wording adjustments annually. In these sessions, it seems like the person who has the most authority or yells the loudest gets their way. Also, the last time we had a new CEO our strategy changed a lot, which caused havoc for some time."

Zack continued, "Know what you mean. Our company's strategic plan appears to be just a bunch of words that any company could be writing. The wording can lead to much interpretation. Also, you know only a few people are involved in setting the strategic course for the whole company. What if the chosen direction is wrong? That could be bad news for the company. I think that we often do not analyze our enterprise data so that we gain true insight into where we should focus our efforts. Perhaps we should have some analytical folks look at the situation differently so that we gain a new perspective before creating these strategic plans. I am concerned that we are directing everyone's measurements and activities to these statements which are not specific and might be unhealthy for the business."

***

As the others continued to talk about their programs and the promise they saw for improvements, Jorge said nothing. He thought that his company didn't need programs. Jorge believed that his people worked hard. He also thought his rapport with his entire management team allowed him to handle problems on a personal level. And he certainly had some problems to work on.

Reduced medical payment schedules had forced Jorge to develop a cost-reduction program within his hospital. After hearing about Hank's problems with his plants in Mexico last month, he had carefully pointed out to his managers that they needed to protect the patients' interests during any cost-reduction initiative. He was confident that the cost reductions wouldn't pose any problems. He had a great pool of talent on his management team, and they were all very committed to their patients.

As they approached the green, Jorge was farthest from the cup. He strode across the green, feeling the springy *give* under his feet that you get on well-maintained golf greens. It was like those rubberized surfaces used for running tracks. He wondered who came up with that idea of combining crushed tires with asphalt to create those spongy track surfaces. He was always fascinated by such creativity and was continually looking for someone with that spark to add to his team.

"Okay," he thought to himself, "back to golf." As he read the break of the green, Zack called out another leader of the free world challenge. If Jorge sank the putt, he could maintain his rule. If not, Zack had an opportunity to become supreme commander on his next putt. Once leadership changed hands, the other could regain power only through another challenge. Jorge was always up for a challenge, especially around the green.

After sinking the 25-footer, Jorge gave Zack a good-natured ribbing for even thinking he could challenge the master. Zack conceded that Jorge was master of the green, for now anyway.

While waiting for the others to putt out, Jorge wondered why Zack never challenged Hank or Wayne. Maybe it was because Jorge and Zack were acknowledged as the best putters in the group. Hank and Wayne were long-ball hitters. They were always giving each other a hard time about a short or missed drive.

It occurred to him that they all seemed to focus their practice on their strengths. Hank and Wayne almost never showed up early on the putting green. They were always at the driving range. Likewise, he never went to the driving range. After thinking about it, he decided that the best way for him to take strokes off his score would be to practice the part of his game that offered the most opportunity for improvement. For him, it wasn't just how far he could hit the ball; it was positioning the ball on the fairway. He had a very good short game, but most of his skill was used to overcome poor ball position after his tee shot.

***

Later, Wayne ruined a routine par hole opportunity with an agonizing four-putt and complained, "I think I'll go buy one of those new one-shot putters that I saw at the clubhouse. I haven't four-putted in years."

Jorge just smiled, remembering some years ago when they were playing regularly. Wayne had bought three new putters in one year to help "fix" his putting. He was still at it.

Just then, everyone jumped when Jorge's cell phone rang. After a brief but animated conversation, Jorge returned to the group. "What's going on, Jorge? I've never seen your face so red," Wayne asked with real concern.

Jorge had a hard time collecting his thoughts. After a moment, he was able to explain his panic in a coherent manner. "There has been a major problem at the hospital. A change in saline bag labeling and sizing caused a whole floor of patients at the hospital to be over-medicated."

He went on, "Doctors are on their way, and I have to head over to help organize our patient protection plan and notification of appropriate government agencies. So far, everyone is okay, thank goodness. However, there are notifications and paper work that have to be handled very carefully to avoid any further allegations of incompetence and cover-up."

Jorge jumped into his cart and headed for the clubhouse as his friends wished him well. They headed for the next tee a lot more somber than they had been just moments ago. Their match was suspended, and they would finish the round without much enthusiasm.

Driving back to the clubhouse, Jorge began collecting his thoughts. He was greatly relieved to hear that none of the over-medications was life threatening. Still this was a very serious problem. How could something like this happen? Who dropped the ball? Jorge thought long and hard on these questions. Was it his fault for pushing for cost reductions? Was it the administrator's fault for notifying only the supervising nurse of the first shift? Was it the nurse's fault for leaving town in the middle of the night to be with her husband who had suffered a heart attack?

Was it the inexperienced nurse who selected the wrong size bag due to a change in labels?

Jorge made it to his car on autopilot, but he was still trying to sort out just what had happened. It seemed like such an unlikely string of events. Why?—How?—he couldn't seem to decide. He was in a painful loop of self-doubt and managerial rage. He decided to put it out of his mind until he got more information at the hospital. After all, there would be plenty of time to try to recover from this mess in the coming weeks.

Jorge tried to focus on the oldies' radio station rather than his current problems. Too bad the music he grew up with was now known as oldies. He started thinking about all the musicians he used to listen to as a young man. It was amazing how many musicians started out and how few found their big break. And for the bands that made it, there was always some interesting story about their hardships along the way.

Didn't all musicians think that they were talented and hard-working? And believe that they would make it? But most didn't. It seemed like it was almost luck of the draw. With so many bands starting, one had to get a break.

Then it hit him like a 300-yard drive right between the eyes. The over-medication was not a fluke event. Having some problem is inevitable; it's just a matter of which problem occurs. There are literally thousands of potentially deadly events that can happen every day in a hospital. All operations, medications, and critical information transfers are like potential musicians trying to get their big break. Some problem will occur sooner or later by chance.

> The over-medication was not a fluke event. Having some problem is inevitable; it's just a matter of which problem occurs.

For any critical activity, there are numerous chains of events that can cause some horrible outcome. Given so many possibilities, even good people doing their jobs well can have problems unless processes are designed to be error-proof. Of course, whenever those problems are reviewed later, the chain of events looks so specific and unusual that everyone believes they were unique occurrences.

Often, we do not recognize that it is the system which allows the failures to take place. The better the system, the less likely a failure will occur. Jorge chastised himself for not realizing this before. In fact, he had presided over task forces that had solved many specific problems. When the task force was finished, the members patted themselves on the back for fixing the problem. They then handled the next problem as though it were an independent issue, missing the system connection between them.

Furthermore, the way the process was set up, all of the obvious high-risk areas had backups. He wondered how many times the backup systems saved a life with no recognition that the backup procedure was even used. After all, if the backup saved someone's life, technically that's still a failure of the original system, costing time and money. Then, with enough failures of the initial process, even the backup systems were likely to fail at some point. There were also other potential issues that might not seem as deadly on the surface, but if you combined a number of failures for these secondary issues, the result might be deadly.

His revelation helped ease his anxiety somewhat; however, having this understanding was still not enough. How could this have been avoided? He kicked himself for not having implemented some type of improvement plan like those of his friends. He hadn't thought he needed it. His problems were different; they were information related.

Now he knew he did need something, but what? The programs his friends were talking about seemed a lot like Wayne's new putter or Zack's new driver. They reminded him of his discussions with his managers: isolated efforts to solve disconnected problems. What he wanted was to change the process of how people did their jobs. That was the only way to head off all the potential failures in the system.

As Jorge pulled into his parking space, he realized he was shaking. This was *his* hospital. These patients were in *his* charge, and *he* was responsible for their well-being. He had almost had a catastrophe, the magnitude of which he didn't want to contemplate.

"All right," he told himself, steadying his hands as they rested on the steering wheel; it ends here. We will change how we do business. Patients will not have to fear for their health when they enter our hospital. And we will still reduce our costs so that we can provide affordable care. Just how this was going to happen he wasn't sure—but it would.

As he climbed out of the car, some doubt started creeping back.

4

Initial Issues

The Short Game

The higher your score, the faster you can lower it—with the short game.

... For two weeks devote 90 percent of your practice time to chipping and putting, and ... your 95 will turn into 90. I guarantee it.

Harvey Penick's Little Red Book (Penick with Shrake 1992)

May

It was mid-morning on a beautiful Saturday. Wayne was sitting outside the Pro Shop at a picnic table, enjoying the cool morning breeze and a cup of coffee. He had arrived at the golf course early to hit some balls at the driving range, and his swing was in fine tune. Now he was just waiting for his friends to arrive. That was the good news. The bad news was that every golfer in the state, it seemed, was either on the course already or in line in front of them. Wayne tried to prepare himself mentally for a long day of slow play. Concentration would be a challenge today. If they had not all been so busy at work, they could have played during the week.

In fact, it had been a long week—a long month for that matter. His management team was working hard to get the Lean Six Sigma program established. They had the newly hired Lean Six Sigma director start putting together some material from their previous TQM program, and develop a new training plan.

He had high hopes for Lean Six Sigma and was disappointed at the response the program generated during its initial six weeks. Earlier in the week, he had visited some of the Lean Six Sigma

training sessions unannounced and found only half of the scheduled managers present.

Engineers and other employees who were required to attend
were unhappy about middle management not buying into the
program. They expressed their concerns openly, worried that
their managers wouldn't know how to utilize Lean Six Sigma
techniques nor understand the time burden it placed on their
employees to complete assigned projects.

Wayne agreed with his employees' concerns and the next day
instituted a sign-in sheet for management. He couldn't believe
he had to resort to this, but attendance did pick up as a result.
However, he wondered if this was really a long-term solution, or
if managers were just going through the motions by attending the
sessions. He certainly hoped his managers were committing to
the program; the company really needed to cut costs and improve
the performance of their over-the-counter health care products.
In the long run, they also needed to reduce development times for
their prescription drugs.

Wayne contemplated his company's loss of market share over
the past couple of years. Marketing had not been able to reverse
the decline, giving excuses that prices were too high.

Jorge and Hank showed up five minutes before their scheduled
tee time, interrupting Wayne's thoughts of future cost reduction
and improvement ideas. No one had heard from Zack, and rather
than giving up their tee time, they proceeded without him, hoping
he could join them later.

***

An hour later, Zack caught up with his friends who were waiting to hit on the fourth tee and engaged in an agitated conversation. Wayne was gesticulating wildly, as Zack arrived just in time
to hear the trailing part of his sentence "… and the managers
weren't even showing up to the training!"

"Hey Zack," Jorge called out, grateful to change the subject,
"Where've you been?"

"I went to the office to take care of some documentation," Zack
replied. "We've been working to implement the balanced scorecard system throughout the company so we can determine where
to focus improvement efforts. It's taken a lot more effort than
expected. Not only that, I think that our fundamental approach
is flawed."

Zack continued, "Let me describe what I mean. A while back, our executive team developed strategies from our corporate vision. From these strategies, we were to establish organizational metrics and goals for these measurements. Let me pull out my strategies cheat-sheet so I can better show you what I mean (see Figure 4.1). Just look at this:

Z-Credit Financial
Strategy

- Develop strategic relationship with industry leaders
- Focus on the development of global logistic capabilities
- Expansion of production capacity
- Achieve further vertical integration
- Maintain technologically advanced and flexible production capabilities
- New products

Figure 4.1: Company strategies.

What do you think about these statements?"

While waiting for their turns at the tee, Wayne and Hank glanced at the pocket-size plastic coated card. Then Wayne said, "These statements could have just as easily been written by my company."

Wayne stopped mid-stride as he was finally stepping onto the tee, turned towards Zack, and proclaimed, "Just had a thought! If I went to classes and some of the team meetings, my managers would know I'm serious about our Lean Six Sigma program."

Wayne launched a slight draw long and down the middle of the fairway, and Zack continued, "We could benefit from red-yellow-green scorecards in that we would have a system where managers throughout the organization react to measurements that are not consistent with our plan. Do you think this could have helped you take care of the type of problem you had last month, Jorge?"

Jorge wasn't listening. Instead, he thought about how this particular hole was easy to play, with a wide fairway that would accommodate the variety of slices and hooks that their foursome usually produced. As luck would have it, he hit the ball straight and long, with just a hint of power-fade. "What do you mean, Zack?" Jorge asked with a smile, obviously pleased with his shot.

"Perhaps you might have built a scorecard that would have highlighted that the change control process for patient medication was not mistake-proof. The only difference between your processes and ours is that ours deal with customers in the financial services industry instead of with medication and patients," Zack explained while lining up to swing.

After Hank and Zack had also hit good shots, they all congratulated each other and started down the fairway. Jorge thought about the unusually good outcome and how many times the four had teed off together over the years. Sooner or later, they were all bound to hit the ball long and straight on the same hole—and this was a rare moment.

Zack continued as they headed down the fairway, "In each of the three divisions where we have started this process there's been a lot of complaining, but we keep telling people we need to understand where to improve so that customers are satisfied, and we meet our strategic goals."

"Have you noticed any improvements yet?" Jorge asked as he walked towards his ball.

"Improvements could take time. We're trying to get our minds around building the scorecards and setting targets for each of them," Zack responded.

Jorge listened intently as he selected a 9 iron to travel the 100 remaining yards to the green. His compact swing was ideal for short-iron play and produced a near-perfect shot with ample backspin that covered the pin placement cut on the front of the green. Jorge's ball landed ten yards beyond and slightly left of the hole, bit on the soft green, hopped backward five feet, and rolled back right towards the pin. Hank yelled, and Wayne ran to get a better look. The ball stopped four inches short of the cup. Zack congratulated Jorge while Hank and Wayne both agreed that it should have gone in.

Jorge was pleased. An eagle on a par 4 would have been a career shot, but he hadn't hit the target. Still, he had come close, and that's what he had wanted to do. He would happily settle for an easy birdie.

***

After his great approach shot, Jorge was able to carry some momentum through the next two holes, where he recorded a par and another birdie on a par 3. He wondered why he was doing so much better on the last few holes. He was wondering if it was luck or real game improvement, when a bogey and a double bogey on the next two holes provided his answer.

With the excitement of golf greatness over, Jorge's thoughts wandered from the game back to work. He wondered why his friends hadn't asked him about the problem that forced him to leave early last time. Perhaps they were each consumed with their own work problems.

Jorge then asked, "So Hank, you haven't spoken much about the Lean program you started. How's it going?"

Hank replied, "Lean looks at the whole value stream. So if your supplier is the reason your deliveries are late, you fix the supplier rather than try to speed up the manufacturing cycle time."

"But to answer your question, it's not going as well as I had hoped. Lean has all of these great tools and approaches. We should be able to use them to reduce costs and lead-time, but I'm not seeing results. I even hired a director of Lean and appointed a steering committee. We recently held a site-wide meeting at the manufacturing plants where this is being implemented."

"You're up, Hank," Wayne said, prodding the group to keep moving. It was easy to get sidetracked when play was slow, he thought.

Hank pulled his driver from his bag, as he explained to his friends some of the problems he was having with Lean. "I went to some training classes and had an experience similar to Wayne's: half the managers weren't in class; they were off fixing problems. When I asked why, they said training was nice when you have time, but they had real work to do." In addition to the buy-in issues, Hank explained, there were problems with spotty implementation. Even where some implementation had taken place, he couldn't see any tangible results.

Wayne grew impatient as he waited for Hank to swing, but Hank continued to discuss the issues he was experiencing with Lean Enterprise. He spoke of the results of various teams. One team conducted some 5S activities, with no visible results. Another team conducted some Kaizen Events. Although this had produced some localized results, Hank could not confirm how the claimed results would impact his business metrics. Optimistically, he told his friends that it would just take some time, and that some of the advanced techniques would have greater impact.

***

The 16th hole was a wicked 527-yard par 5 with a double dogleg and a creek that crossed the fairway twice. Trees on both sides of the tight fairway gave weekend golfers plenty of chances to shed old golf balls.

While the group waited, Zack noticed that Jorge was about to tee off with a 3 iron. When asked why, Jorge answered with a sly grin, "I haven't hit a driver all day long!"

"But what about that great drive on number 4 that set you up for the birdie?" asked Hank.

"That was my 3 wood," Jorge smiled. "I'm tired of fighting my game. I don't want to have to make difficult second shots continually to save a hole after a bad tee shot gets me in trouble. I used some Wisdom of the Organization to list out the reasons for my bad holes and decided that it was my erratic driver."

Wayne laughed, "Wisdom of the Organization? What's that?"

"It's a term I learned from the Integrated Enterprise Excellence training I've been going through at work," Jorge replied. "In our IEE training, we were taught how Wisdom of the Organization comes intuitively from what you know about a process due to past experience. At work, we use Wisdom of the Organization to come up with ideas on how to improve our business processes. I just evaluated my golf game using my own Wisdom of the Organization based on past experience. My biggest problem seems to be my tee shots. Bad tee shots are killing me. It doesn't matter how good my short game is; too often, my drives are bad enough that I can't recover. I decided to leave my driver in the bag today, and I've had only one double bogey."

Zack questioned, "But Jorge, you hit some good drives, too."

Jorge elaborated, "I looked at the distribution of my drives in both distance and accuracy. Over the last ten years I have played over 300 rounds of golf. When I really thought about it, fewer than 20% of my drives are really good enough to get me in position to make par or birdie. About two-thirds of them leave me in some degree of trouble, and on about half of them, I can salvage a par or bogey with my good short game. The other half the time I have to struggle just to save bogey. The rest of my tee shots are so bad that even my short game can't save me and I'm facing double bogey or worse. By making smarter decisions on my tee shots, I may be a little shorter off the tee, but I'm more predictable. I can plan my attack better, and reduce the chances of falling apart on a hole. I guess you could say that I've made my process more robust."

Zack said, "What do you mean? Have you been working out?"

Jorge laughed and said, "No, I guess you could say I am just working 'smarter.' The term 'robust' refers to the concept of picking a process, in this case the club I hit, that has a normal variation pattern well within the allowable limits for the task. You are familiar with mistake-proofing, of course. Well, when we can't mistake-proof the process completely, the next best thing is to be robust. In golf, that means picking the club that has the highest probability of landing in an acceptable spot with respect to both direction and distance. If my 3 iron has a 90% chance of keeping me in play for par, and my driver only has a 30% chance of doing that, my process for making good drives is more robust with the 3 iron. Even if the driver gives me a slightly better chance for birdie by going farther, it has a much higher chance of going into a hazard or out-of-bounds. 'Course management' is at least partially 'risk management.' It depends on the situation."

With that, Jorge hit his 3 iron off the tee, 175 yards down the middle, just short of the creek, in good position for his second shot.

Zack looked incredulous, "Where did you come up with all this?"

"Our IEE training inspired this change," said Jorge.

Wayne interrupted, "IEE? What's that?"

"IEE is short for Integrated Enterprise Excellence. Wayne, you are now implementing Lean Six Sigma, right?"

"Yep," Wayne responded.

"Hank, you are implementing Lean, right?"

"Sure are," Hank responded.

"Zack, you are building the balanced scorecard system from your strategies, right?"

"Yes, we are," Zack replied.

Jorge continued, "There are aspects of all these systems that are great. For example, having scorecard balance is what you want. Concentrating on profits and disregarding customer satisfaction can lead to disaster. A scorecard balance should address both profit and voice of the customer. If Hank would focus only on making on-time deliveries but ignored WIP, his company's inventories could go through the roof causing major financial issues. Hank's organization should have a scorecard balance that addresses both on-time delivery and WIP. Care needs to be exercised in not only defining but also monitoring the balanced scorecard metrics. Some organizations create the balanced scorecard metrics through a strategic plan that did not formally address their organizational value chain. This can lead to metrics that drive the wrong kind of behavior."

Hank interjected, "I can relate to that. Our metrics regularly lead to the wrong behavior."

Jorge continued, "IEE uses components from all your systems to take Lean Six Sigma and the balanced scorecard to their next level. For example, in IEE the value chain metrics are to be selected so that there is scorecard metric balance; however, the IEE system for tracking these metrics is different. Basically, the IEE metric tracking system can reduce organizational firefighting.

"Let me give you a little background about the overall IEE system. As I am sure it was pointed out in Wayne's deployment, Six Sigma was started by Motorola and made popular by GE. Some companies have dramatically impacted their bottom-line through the completion of projects. The people who drive these projects are called black belts."

"Black belts? Is this some kind of martial art?" Zack interrupted again. He grinned as he noticed that Hank seemed to like that idea.

Jorge continued, "No, black belts are trained to work with teams and tackle problems systematically. After the over-medication problem we had last month, I knew we had to do something different. I had read some articles about the benefits of Lean Six Sigma and decided to do some investigating. There has been a lot of pro and con discussion about the success of Lean Six Sigma. Even the cartoon Dilbert gives Six Sigma a blow from time to time.

"In an Internet search, I discovered an IEE alternative that integrates the strengths and down plays the weakness of many techniques including Six Sigma, Lean, and the balanced scorecard."

> I then discovered an IEE alternative that integrates the strengths and down plays the weakness of many techniques including Six Sigma, Lean, and balanced scorecards. Unlike these project-driven systems, IEE is more of an overall business system for both measurements and improvements

Jorge calmly stood over his second shot, and split the fairway a second time with another beautiful 3 iron, that went 170 yards, stopping well short of the second creek crossing, right in the opening of the dogleg for his approach to the green.

"Are you doing this on your own or having a company help with your deployment?" Wayne asked.

"We are using an outside company to help us with our deployment."

Wayne quickly interjected, "You are smart. We were penny wise and pound foolish when we tried hiring someone who was trained in Lean Six Sigma and then tried to implement the system ourselves. You should be able to get things going a lot quicker using the resources of an organization outside your company. It is important to partner up with a provider that fits well with your company. This is not the right time to try to save money by selecting someone who is local or using a university course."

Jorge continued, "I found a couple books that had a step-by-step process for IEE implementation. Like Wayne, at first I thought we could use these books to implement IEE on our own. After further investigation, I realized we needed expert advice to get started. The company we went with did not simply focus on doing projects. They focused on how to create an overall business system of measurements and improvements that helps organizations move toward the three Rs of business: everyone doing the Right things and doing them Right at the Right time. In addition, they had the detailed roadmaps to accomplish this. This overall system could be used by executive management to improve organizational governance"

When they reached Jorge's ball, he hit a *third* perfect 3 iron to within a few yards of the front of the green. After some delay looking for Zack's ball in the left rough, they finally made their way to the green.

When it was Jorge's turn, he smoothly chipped his 7 iron into the front of the green and rolled it to within eight inches of the cup. Hank, who had hit a monster 285-yard drive, had hooked his approach shot into the trees and scrambled for a bogey. Wayne hit two beautiful shots and a half wedge onto the green before three-putting again for a bogey. Zack's ball went unfound in the trees, and with the penalty strokes took an eight.

As they waited on the 17th tee, Jorge finished his story. "When I decided to go with IEE, I learned that success is dependent upon organizational understanding and buy-in at all levels. Our deployment consultant provided a system to accomplish this in a one-week workout. The first day of the workout week had a hands-on workshop that described the methodology and how this system would resolve many organizational pains that routinely occur.

"This session described an enterprise process define-measure-analyze-improve-control system, or E-DMAIC. This E-DMAIC system serves as an orchestration infrastructure for defining your organization's value chain with a unique measurement tracking and reporting system. The IEE system of measurements has many advantages over a red-yellow-green scorecard approach. In addition, there is a structured enterprise analyze phase that leads to the structured building of strategies and projects that are in direct alignment to over-business goal objectives. This system offers the framework for a true integration of analytics with innovation."

> This E-DMAIC system serves as an orchestration infrastructure for defining your organization's value chain with a unique measurement tracking and reporting system. The IEE system of measurements has many advantages over a red-yellow-green scorecard approach. Unlike these project-driven systems, IEE is more of an overall business system for both measurements and improvements

"On the second through the fourth day of the week, our IEE deployment consultant worked directly with our technical team roughing out our company's overall E-DMAIC structure. On the fifth day, the executive team was brought back in for a two-hour presentation. In this presentation, the executive team saw the first build of our tailored system. They were impressed. In addition to describing this new system, this presentation highlighted how many of our current practices were encouraging firefighting and leading to the wrong activities. We are now preparing to conduct champion training."

Zack interrupted, "What are champions?"

Jorge continued, "Champions are executive managers who remove barriers that black belts encounter while executing their projects. Unlike traditional Lean Six Sigma deployments where you might train 20 black belts, our deployment consultant suggests starting small with the best people and grows the infrastructure into a larger system. We are now training six black belts at our deployment consultant's facility. This training consists of four one-week training sessions that are conducted over four months. Each trainee has a project that is in true alignment with the business goals and is worth at least $100,000 to the business. Our deployment consultant not only provides on-site project coaching but also coaching on the refinement of our overall E-DMAIC system, which was roughed out in the one-week workout.

"Defining and scoping-out projects are essential. In a traditional Lean Six Sigma deployment, management might simply decide what major functions were most critical, what specific processes within the functions were important, and how to track the key process output variables or KPOVs of the process. These managers could be right or they might be wrong. Some organizations have claimed 100 million dollars in savings but nobody can seem to find the money. The IEE system has a different approach where value chain metric improvement needs pull for the project creation.

"Like everyone else, we're having some buy-in problems. This system is transitioning our organization from firefighting activities to fire preventive actions. This is uncomfortable for some people since their rise to the organization's top was because they were good firefighters. The cultural transition to being more data driven will be healthy for us."

As the group waited on the 18th tee, Hank thought for a minute, and then said, "Maybe I should leave my driver in the bag, and avoid my double bogeys too."

Jorge smiled and said, "All of our games are different. Before you decide on your game improvement method, you really need to measure and analyze your own game. I'm sure you'll find that, on many holes, your driver is a formidable weapon. You just need to understand the percentages."

Then Hank said, "At least, I think I'll check out your IEE methods. Can you get me started?"

"Sure," Jorge responded.

On the 18th green, Jorge snaked in a ten-foot side-hill putt for 79! It was his best score in several years, and his driver had never left the bag. He even beat Wayne, who shot 80.

Jorge said, "I want to get something out of my car. I'll catch up with you in the clubhouse. Hold off ordering drinks until I get there. I want to buy the first round."

Jorge hurriedly walked to his car. He opened the trunk and picked a folder from inside his briefcase. Before meeting his friends at their favorite table, Jorge stopped by the bar and gave the bartender the folder.

Jorge bought a round, and said, "When I was doing my web search that located information about IEE, I also found a couple articles that I think you will find very interesting."

Just then the server returned to the table and said, "Sam, the bartender, wanted me to give you these copies."

Jorge responded, "Thanks."

As Jorge handed out two articles to each friend he said, "This article from '21 Common Problems (and What to Do about Them)' [see Appendix Section A.1] nets out many traditional Six Sigma or Lean Six Sigma deployment issues. You can look over the article in detail later. But, for now, let's look at the first of the twenty-one listed common problems: *My organization started its Lean Six Sigma deployment five years ago, and now we're having difficulty finding projects, especially projects of value."*

Hank interrupted, "This does not seem possible."

Jorge continued, "Know what you mean. However, I understand that when companies push or hunt for projects to create it is not uncommon for this to occur. I have discovered that IEE not only addresses these issues but is also much more than a project-driven system, like Lean Six Sigma. IEE is an overall business system for both organizational measurements and improvements.

"The second article 'Starting a Six Sigma Initiative' (see Appendix Section A.2) describes issues that should be addressed in a Lean Six Sigma and IEE deployment. Look at the first question response. The article says, *'full deployment is often suggested as the best way to initiate Six Sigma; however, it is typically better to grow into an overall system. In the real world, most companies don't have the bandwidth to create an infrastructure that can support a very large instantaneous Six Sigma deployment.'* This article describes some IEE basics, which improves upon the Lean Six Sigma deployment system found in many companies."

As they were getting ready to leave they all agreed that it had been a very long day, almost a six-hour round, but somehow, everyone felt like it just may have been worth it.

5

Continuing Problems

One of many wonderful things about golf...

Like chess, golf is a game that is forever challenging but can never be conquered.

Harvey Penick's Little Red Book (Penick with Shrake 1992)

August

It was late on a hot, muggy Friday night in August, on the eve of the monthly golf game. Zack sat sulking in his office. Why couldn't he figure out why customer complaints were still going *up?* True to his nature, when things started going badly, Zack took personal responsibility for fixing the problem. However, it seemed as if every time he and his team fixed one problem, several new ones would appear to take its place. It was as if he were trapped watching continuous reruns of the old movie *Gremlins.* Every time they killed off a defect, several unpleasant little relatives seemed to reappear. The thought of skipping the monthly golf outing with his old college buddies crossed his mind, but he hated it. Because of vacations and weddings, the foursome hadn't met since May, and he was way past ready for a little break.

Z-Credit Financial had recently developed a system to capture customer complaints and respond within 24 hours with an action plan for closure. Then, when complaints continued to come in, Zack dove into the details of the tracking system. He was trying to assess whether people had really been conducting root-cause analysis and were following up on action items. It seemed like the proper procedures were being followed, and yet wrong addresses and incorrect balance transfers were still frequently occurring defects.

Zack wondered why his implementation of the balanced score-card program hadn't led to fewer customer complaints. There was always something else going wrong, and overall, things were not improving. At one in the morning, he found his coffee-pot empty and decided to give the investigation up for the night. He tried to think how he could start fresh in the morning and knew for sure that he would be missing another round with his friends.

On the drive home, Zack's mind wandered toward the golf game he would be missing tomorrow. Jorge's magical round was the last real success story he could remember. Maybe Wayne was wrong. Maybe he didn't need a new driver. Maybe he should change the way he approached the game, and leave the driver in the bag like Jorge. But what about all the other shots that got him in trouble? Whenever he worked on one part of his game, defects popped up in other areas to kill his round. What had Jorge said to Hank at the end of his round? He said something about each of them hav-ing different games and the need to analyze your own game before deciding on an improvement strategy.

As Zack entered the driveway of his home, he noted that the lights were out. Liz and the kids had finally given up and gone to bed. The cold supper in the fridge and the dark house didn't seem like the payback he was hoping for. Maybe if he got started early tomorrow, he could still salvage some time with his family on Sunday.

***

During the last two months, Hank had also been experiencing problems with his Lean program. One implementation team was able to reduce batch size on one of the manufacturing lines, but defects caused confusion and problems to the point that there was actually more work-in-progress (WIP) inventory than when they had started. Some of the process cycle times had improved, but the overall cycle time to get a part through the system has increased considerably. Several of his key customers were now reminding him that the real business metrics were established and measured by the customer.

On another process, a Kaizen Event was conducted in order to reduce manufacturing costs for a particular product by addressing the setup time for a sheet metal punching operation.

The team was able to reduce setup time from an average of two hours to 15 minutes by setting up the punches outside the press. Even though there were hidden problems with increased labor costs, the team truly believed that they were successful because setup time was reduced. Hank knew that the overall business improvement was negligible so far, but he hoped that even a perceived success might motivate his team.

Hank felt like he was back calling the defensive plays in college again. Whenever he moved people up to stop the run, the opponent would pass. When he dropped back into coverage, the opposition ran over them. When Hank decided to blitz from his linebacker slot, they would dump a screen pass over his head. He needed a better system then, and he needed one now. He hadn't been able to talk to Jorge since their last round, but now he was eager to know more about Jorge's systems approach to improvement, both for business and for golf.

***

Meanwhile, Wayne had growing concerns about his Lean Six Sigma deployment as well. Two projects were finished and the reported financial savings were good, but he was not sure that the problems they had solved really impacted the overall company's financials. A lot more projects were coming up, but he was not sure of their business value either. Overall customer satisfaction had not improved, and teams were not spending enough time on their projects. Wayne had been burning a lot of midnight oil trying, in vain, to determine why Lean Six Sigma had not given him the results he expected. The teams were well organized, and seemed to be motivated, but they just couldn't seem to see the key relationships between the processes that they could control and the business outcomes they needed.

Wayne removed his glasses and rubbed his eyes. On these long days, he could hardly read the detail reports, let alone see any key process relationships. He was getting a headache. Maybe he needed new glasses. Karen had been pestering him about having his eyes checked. He'd make that appointment as soon as he got over the hump at work. Too bad he didn't know anyone who could give his Lean Six Sigma program a vision check. His mind drifted toward his family. Karen was a great mom to Mike and Shelly. It had to be tough now that they were both teenagers. He needed to spend more time with all of them. He really needed to get this

Lean Six Sigma program running under its own power. Wonder-Chem needed more results, and his family needed more of him.

***

Unlike his friends, Jorge was making significant progress with his IEE business strategy. Monthly status meetings now had metric report-outs that mean something. He found in the past they had been wasting much time fighting phantom issues. Several of the teams had found some unexpected low-hanging-fruit opportunities for improvement. Even better, these projects were well aligned with the financial business goals, making the project benefits even more visible. This seemed to excite and motivate other teams to work even harder on their projects as well. Some real momentum was building.

Personally, Jorge was elated with the results. He learned that some of the statistical analyses his teams were doing had indicated there were many common-cause issues intrinsic to their processes. Previously, these issues would probably have been interpreted as special causes, events unusual to the process. Fire-fighting would have ensued, and often the almost random fixes would have masked real root causes and may have made overall system performance worse. Now, his teams were able to pinpoint those areas where overall system improvement was required, and have a better idea how to proceed. Jorge's organization recently created metrics for Harris Hospital that separated common cause from special cause. Now his teams were learning how to make long-lasting improvements through fixing the process, not just firefighting the problem of the day.

> Previously, these issues would probably have been interpreted as special causes, events unusual to the process. Fire-fighting would have ensued, and often the almost random fixes would have masked real root causes and may have made overall system performance worse.

Jorge leaned back as he visualized how an IEE perspective could apply to many additional areas of his business. He could see the way that improvements-through-projects were affecting how his people viewed their processes in terms of the overall business results. The thought of expanding it throughout the business was exciting. Jorge, always the system thinker, thought this was a great business improvement system.

Jorge stretched and relaxed for a moment, thinking about dinner tonight and golf tomorrow. He deserved a break, and tonight's dinner with Sandra should be a great start to a good weekend. He was taking Sandra to their favorite place, a quiet little restaurant they had found when they first met. Thinking about Sandra made him smile. She was a beautiful lady and a very successful career woman. He'd learned so much from her. When he was studying pre-med, he had learned to reason in the logical/analytical style of a scientist. Later, his MBA classes taught him to think in terms of business systems. But when he met Sandra, he was amazed to find her to be very successful even though she seemed to rely almost entirely on her powerful intuition and understanding of human nature. Over the years, their discussions had taught him that his logic did not always lead to the right answer, and that Sandra was right at least as often as he was. Now he relied on her wonderful intuitive senses to augment his logic and systems thinking. Together, they made quite a team.

His mind wandered a bit further, thinking about creativity and wondering if that was what *thinking out of the box* was really about: suspending traditional logic and analyses long enough to consider possibilities that did not seem to compute logically. He thought about the many times as a scientist and businessman that he had seen long-accepted theories disproved in favor of new illogical theories. Yes, he decided, good business management is a combination of science and logic, business and finance, and people's creativity and intuition. The trick was to treat it as a system.

6

The Discussion

The Three Most Important Clubs

... the three most important clubs in the bag, in order, [are the] putter, the driver, and the wedge.

A good putter is a match for anyone.   A bad putter is a match for no one.

Harvey Penick's Little Red Book (Penick with Shrake 1992)

August

Hank and Jorge stood alone near the first tee early Saturday morning. "Too bad about Zack and Wayne," Jorge lamented. "At least these two fellows they paired us with look like they can hit the ball."

"You would think Zack and Wayne could get out for a round of golf," Hank replied sarcastically. He didn't know if he was mad at them for not showing up or for working while he was playing. He worried about the time away from the office and wondered if he should be working as well.

As they waited to tee off, Hank started thinking about IEE. He was impressed with Jorge's success with the program and was wondering if it might complement his Lean program. Hank remembered what Jorge had told him at the last outing, specifically that IEE was not a program, but a statistically based business system and improvement methodology, which improves how operations are measured and improved. Jorge was emphatic about IEE's equating to how people *should* do their jobs, especially at the executive level. Since the last outing, Hank

45

had been doing his homework and had a lot of questions for Jorge.

"I thought the articles you gave us (see Appendix) were very insightful. I have done some additional reading and now see what you mean that IEE has many Lean Six Sigma components. It seems like everybody says that Lean Six Sigma is just for engineers to reduce defects, inventory, or lead times on manufacturing processes. Is the major goal of the Six Sigma component to achieve 3.4 defects per million operations or something called DPMO? Is this also the goal of IEE?" Hank asked.

Jorge responded, "That's what you often hear about Six Sigma. The DPMO or "defects per million opportunities" metric was created by engineers. Each Six Sigma project problem statement is to have a defect definition which is to be improved by the project. A process that has a 3.4 DPMO rate is said to be at a Six Sigma quality level.

"One difference between IEE and Six Sigma is that IEE does not require a defect definition for projects. This is a very important distinction. Think about a project that is to reduce invoice days sales outstanding or WIP. What is a true defect definition for these two situations?"

> One difference between IEE and Six Sigma is that IEE does not require a defect definition for projects.

Hank said, "Only goals can be set for these situations. There are no true specifications like the dimension on a part."

"Agreed. Establishing goals so that you can calculate a defective or DPMO rate makes no sense. I don't like it when measurements have subjectivity like this. This can lead to playing games with the numbers. For example, if I want an improved sigma quality level, I could simply adjust my goal.

"As we discussed in a previous golf outing, IEE roadmaps include most, if not all, of the tools and techniques that you are using in your deployment. IEE includes Lean methods in both the E-DMAIC roadmap and improvement project execution roadmap, which is called P-DMAIC. In addition, both roadmaps include a lot of statistical measures and methods that apply to both manufacturing and transactional situations. These statistical tools and methods help us to improve our business measures, prioritize what's important, better understand our current important processes, evaluate potential solutions, and make sure that the improvement holds.

"What role do managers play in the success of IEE?" Hank wondered aloud.

"As part of the E-DMAIC analyze phase, improvement targets are established for various manager owned process. For example, a business goal to improve profit margins by 1% could lead to a plant manager defective rate reduction target of 10%. This manager would then assign a black belt to this value chain metric P-DMAIC project.

"Management's task is to create the infrastructure, remove barriers, and make improvements happen," Jorge continued. "When you asked the computer components group to cut costs, you expected the individual managers to reduce their expenditures, reduce head count, cut discretionary spending, and reduce inventory. Standard stuff, right? With this type of thinking you were set up to fail sooner or later. People worked independently within their own responsibilities trying to solve the problem. Nobody was looking at the bigger picture, which resulted in havoc for your Mexico operations."

Hank listened intently as he took his driver from the bag. He settled in to his pre-shot routine, and took a smooth but powerful swing. The results drew positive exclamations from Jorge and the two new partners, as a long drive with just a hint of draw pierced the fairway. Hank worried silently for an instant that he might have hit it too well, and gone through the slight dogleg into the first cut of rough.

"If you had a team that approached this as a systems issue, a more effective solution could have been found. The problem may have been prevented instead of corrected after it occurred. A broader picture could have offered a bigger and more permanent solution. Black belts are trained to start with a very broad view and work their way toward the details," Jorge continued as they approached Hank's drive.

"I don't believe it!" Hank yelled from a couple feet away.

"No, it's true," replied Jorge, astonished at his friend's harsh reaction.

"Oh no, no," laughed Hank. "I was talking about my lie; I'm almost buried in this rough. How can the first cut be this thick?" He pulled a 5 iron from his bag as he said, "If I can get out of this rough in one stroke, it will be a miracle. Actually, I'm interested in hearing the rest if you don't mind me stealing your ideas."

"Why did you pick that club?" Jorge asked, seemingly more interested in Hank's club selection.

Hank responded, "I'm about 170 from the pin. My 5 iron normally goes a bit farther than that, but I expect to have trouble getting out of this buried lie."

"Yes, don't you normally hit your 5 iron more like 185 or 190?" Jorge questioned. Without waiting for an answer he continued, "Remember my decision to leave the driver in the bag last time? I did that to minimize the variation in my tee shots, so I could predict where I would land more accurately. Through better club selection, I can make my shot process more robust to the normal variability in my swing. With this approach, I could depend on good ball positioning to make pars or save bogeys. If you hit that 5 iron cleanly, you'll go over the green into the trees. If you don't, you won't reach it anyway, and you'll land in one of the front sand traps."

"OK," Hank said with a flash of interest, "what do you suggest?"

Jorge offered, "If you hit a 9 iron, you will almost certainly get out of the rough and land in the open area just in front of the green. Then pitch on close and make your putt for par. You're looking at a tap-in for bogey five, worst case. But if you leave that 5 iron in the rough, or pull it into the trees, you're on your way to another eight. What do you think?"

"Or maybe I should have hit my 3 iron off the tee, stayed short of the dogleg, and hit my 5 iron to the green in the first place?" Hank added.

"That would have been good, too, but now that you're here, make the best of it. Plan ahead and keep the overall goal in mind. It's not always about maximizing the current shot at any cost. Remember, they don't ask *how* at the end of the day, just *how many*?" said Jorge.

After Hank hit a solid 9 iron to within 20 yards of the front of the green, Jorge continued, "I was thinking about the problems you had in Mexico. An IEE solution wouldn't even have started with your statement that you wanted to reduce costs by moving operations. First, you start with ... better yet, let me draw you a picture (see Figure 6.1).

"Note how this picture describes a quite different approach from the balanced scorecard approach used by Zack, which starts with the creation of strategies. With the balanced scorecard approach, strategies lead to metrics that are consistent with the strategies. In IEE, the value chain describes what your company does. Metrics then describe how well your organization executes these functions in a time-series fashion, where common-cause

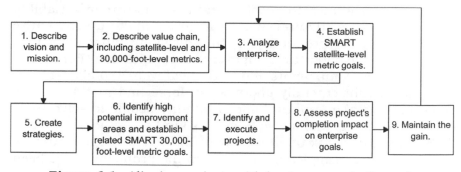

Figure 6.1: Aligning projects with business needs through E-DMAIC roadmap.

variability is separated from special-cause variability. Note that these metrics are not really dependent upon your strategies.

"Collins (2001) describes in *Good to Great* a level five leader as someone who is not only great when they are leading an organization but also the organization remains great after the person is no longer affiliated with it. A level-five-leader-created legacy could be described as being a *Level Five System.* In our workshop, the instructor asked this question: 'Do you think that your organization's strategy would change if there were different leadership?' Everyone in our workshop responded positively to the question. The instructor then asked if it 'Wouldn't be reasonable to conclude that it would be very difficult for an organization to create a Level Five System when the primary guiding light for the organization is its strategy, which can change with new leadership?' We all agreed.

"For an organization, value chain improvements should be made over time; however, the fundamental value chain structure and its metrics would be fundamentally independent from the organization's strategy. In IEE, strategies are to be developed after formulation of the organizational value chain, its metrics, and an enterprise analysis. Because of this, the overall organizational structure can maintain continuity between leadership changes. IEE can become the enabling system to create a level five organization.

"In IEE executives communicate organizational goals. Teams are then to work on projects that are aligned with these goals. Suppose that the cost reduction was the most important problem and you assigned a team to attack the issue. They wouldn't start to reduce costs by studying the individual budgets of the groups involved. Rather, they would ask a number of questions. How do we define and measure cost? What is the nature of variability within our cost structure? What categories make up the entire cost structure for production in this division? What categories offer the greatest opportunity for overall cost reduction? For a given category, what components add to that category's total cost?"

Hank thought carefully about what Jorge had just said, "I've been thinking about all the times I told my people to solve some huge problem and didn't give them this kind of a process to make the job doable. Think of all the opportunities for huge returns if we get some of these teams on the chronic problems we've been firefighting for ever."

> I've been thinking about all the times I told my people to solve some huge problem and didn't give them this kind of a process to make the job doable.

Hank was good with his wedge. It was a strong point in his game. He hit a pretty pitch shot that landed on the front of the green and rolled to within four feet of the flag. With his confidence up, he drilled his par putt and then asked Jorge the big question, "So I should start teeing off regularly with my 3 iron?"

Jorge laughed, "Of course not. Your big drives are a great weapon in your arsenal. But golf is a target game—distance *and* direction. Think about the target area that you need to hit with each shot. What are the limits of acceptable errors in distance and direction? Then pick the best club to hit. Not by the longest distance you have ever hit it, but the range of distances you normally hit it. And don't forget the range of direction errors you normally make. For your driver, I'd bet most of your shots travel 220 to 280 yards."

With this, he handed Hank a picture he had just drawn on the back of the scorecard. It was the familiar normal distribution with a mean at 250 yards and standard deviation partitions marked off in 15-yard increments (see Figure 6.2). Jorge then said, "Plus and minus two sigma only cover about 95% of your drives, and 205 to 295 would cover 99.74%. Your 370-yarder last year was a pleasant 'outlier.' These are just estimates, of course. You can refine them with measurement and analysis. But if you had thought about the likelihood associated with various driving distances, you might not have selected a driver back there where the far side of the dogleg was only 260 yards away."

"Of course," Hank's insight flashed. "I should think of my golf swing as a process where key process outputs that I want to

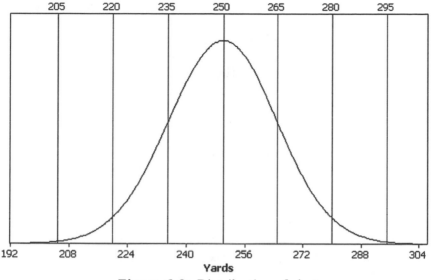

Figure 6.2: Distribution of shots.

control are distance and accuracy. A key process input variable to this process is choice of clubs. For my swing, each club produces a distribution of shots with a range of distance and directional accuracy. I should pick the club most likely to give the best response for each operation... I mean shot."

"Now you've got it," smiled Jorge. "There will be times when you have plenty of open space and your driver will be a terrific weapon. Just pick your spots wisely."

***

Later, Jorge said, "In IEE there are a couple of underlying principles that all employees can use within their job to improve their efficiency. First, they need to understand the big picture. Next they need to know what the customer wants, both internal and external customers. They also need to reduce variation and drive to target."

"Didn't you say something about this is the way people should do their jobs? Until now, we've been discussing teams that go after specific problems. Where does the continuous improvement come in?" asked Hank.

"These ideas can be used to improve your company's processes on an ongoing basis without causing chaos like you experienced in Mexico. It's pretty clear that the manager didn't understand the big picture or the voice of the customer when he made the decision to change plants on the basis of component cost alone."

Hank agreed as he looked at the picture on the back of the scorecard again at the next tee. Then he looked at the hole and saw a small landing area for the drive that was only about 30 yards in diameter, about 200 yards from the tee. He reached for his 4 iron as Jorge smiled.

"Take my business," Jorge continued. "Our customer service representatives (CSRs) are supposed to keep track of patients' billing records. Historically, we had CSRs separated by functional area: Each would work in emergency, hospital or physical therapy. It seemed like a natural way to do it because each CSR would become familiar and efficient with the area-specific procedures. After taking two weeks of IEE training, one of our less-experienced CSRs suggested we combine CSRs into one functional area. This would allow all CSRs to see how each area addresses issues, allow us to back each other up, and actually reduce head count by five employees."

"That's amazing!" Hank commented. "Why would someone make a suggestion that could put him out of work?"

"Because up front we personally assured everyone that any improvements would not result in the loss of jobs. We explained we would retrain displaced workers to enhance their skills. Job reductions would only occur through normal attrition. The worker that made the suggestion was re-trained for an area we knew was going to need people in the near future."

"This sounds great, Jorge, but you haven't really told me how this works. I would need to hear more of the details about the infrastructure and how the project teams function. And what about Lean? Was that a waste of my time? How about TQM, Baldrige, and ISO-9000, for that matter? How do they fit in? What do you know about Theory of Constraints or TOC? Does that fit in with your IEE system too?"

"Tell you what, Hank. I'll explain the IEE connection with other programs while I take you on for the rest of the round. During lunch, I'll lay out some of the basics of the IEE infrastructure and project execution. Remember, I've only been at this for about three months now, so I don't know all the details, but I can give you the big picture."

"Sounds great," Hank said. "Now, what about the connection between Six Sigma and Lean?"

"Actually, Hank, I've heard different answers to this question. It depends on whom you ask. Most companies that start with

Lean believe that you do Lean first which leads to the application of Six Sigma tools to reduce defects. Six Sigma proponents often say it works the other way round. They tend to believe that after Six Sigma is implemented, you can address workflow issues using Lean methodologies.

"IEE has a different spin on things. The IEE system provides a high-level scorecard or dashboard for business financial and operational metrics, which has no calendar boundaries such as quarter or year. Business financial measures are tracked as satellite-level metrics. Operational and project measures are tracked as 30,000-foot-level metric. Using the satellite-level metric strategy, businesses track measures like return on investment and gross revenue on a monthly basis. As part of this strategy, the 30,000-foot-level metrics could track project or operational metrics such as defective rates, WIP, or lead times on a daily basis and are designed to get you out of the firefighting mode."

> The IEE system provides a high-level scorecard or dashboard for business financial and operational metrics, which has no calendar boundaries such as quarter or year. Business financial measures are tracked as satellite-level metrics. Operational and project measures are tracked as 30,000-foot-level metric.

Hank responded, "Sounds great!"

Jorge continued, "The purpose of the 30,000-foot-level chart is to view a process response from a high-level, airplane view to determine whether a process is predictable. That is, the process has common-cause variability. If the process output from common-cause variability is not satisfactory, or what we desire, then a process improvement project would be pulled for creation. That is, you need to systematically improve the overall process, rather than chasing daily problems. The tools you select to fix the process depend on your situation. If the problem were from waste or muda, you would probably use Lean tools. Other situations require Six Sigma tools, and some even require both."

> The purpose of the 30,000-foot-level chart is to view a process response from a high-level, airplane view to determine whether a process is predictable. That is, the process has common-cause variability. If the process output from common cause variability is not satisfactory or what we desire, then a process improvement project would be pulled for creation.

"What about Kaizen Events?" Hank asked.

"People often include these techniques in their Lean implementation. Our instructor described one company, which said that they did a Kaizen Event every other week and saved $10,000 per event. This might initially sound impressive, but do you think it's real?"

Hank paused for a moment, "If the boss told me to save $10,000 per event, I bet I could make it look like I did."

Jorge responded, "Exactly! However, what happened during the Kaizen Event might be detrimental to the entire system. For example, one cell could have improved its efficiency and piled excess inventory in front of the next cell of the process, creating a bottleneck. At the end of the day, the overall system was degraded for localized gain.

"The 30,000-foot-level metric view of a process can lead to Kaizen Events when appropriate. A process for executing Kaizen Events is part of the P-DMAIC improve phase. This approach keeps you from spending a lot of time and money on Kaizen Events that don't benefit the overall business."

Hank persisted with his questions, asking, "Where does TOC fit in?"

"Theory of Constraints is part of the E-DMAIC analyze phase. TOC can identify and model constraint areas that need improvement through P-DMAIC projects. Have you really considered the impact of identifying organizational constraints and taking action on them?"

After a hesitation, Hank said, "I have been too busy fighting fires that I have not had a chance to do much of anything."

"Jorge continued, "Consider that a manufacturing operation can sell everything that it can make. If you are able to identify a constraint and improve its operational capacity by three percent, all the gross revenue from additional product sales, less raw material costs, goes directly to the bottom line since fix costs have already been covered."

Hank responded, "Wow, when you think about it that could be big bucks. Sounds like we could also use IEE to meet our ISO-9000:2000 requirements as well. With the 2000 version of ISO-9000, we now not only have to document our processes but we also have to show that we're improving them."

"The question is what do you do? Do you need to improve all your processes or just the critical ones?" Jorge asked.

"I certainly wouldn't want to try to improve everything. Some areas just aren't as important as others and don't need improvement," Hank replied.

"The great thing about this is you could reference your IEE Business Strategy as the methodology for improving your organization per the ISO-9000:2000 requirement. With this approach, you can leverage your improvement activities to the needs of the business," Jorge added.

"What about the people who say Six Sigma, and I would assume IEE too, is just TQM repackaged?" Hank wondered.

"TQM is different. Typically, TQM was set up as a separate entity within an organization to solve quality problems. Lean Six Sigma focus has been to execute projects, where most projects were to have validated financial benefits. IEE is more than a project executing methodology. IEE is an enterprise system for orchestrating business activities, including measurements and improvements, which truly impact the bottom line." Jorge explained.

"I have this twenty-foot putt for a birdie to win today's round. I believe you'll be buying lunch, or would you rather put the leadership of the free world on this?" Hank commented as he stroked the downhill putt through two breaks and into the cup.

Hank turned with a satisfied grin and headed to the clubhouse. As he walked off, he heard Jorge call after him, "That's another premise of IEE: if you putt enough times, you're bound to make one sooner or later. Even a blind squirrel finds an acorn once in a while."

7

It's in the Details

The Average Golfer

... sometimes I wonder, what is an average golfer?

I read somewhere that ... the average male golfer shoots about 92.

I don't believe it. Not if he counts every stroke and plays by USGA rules.

Harvey Penick's Little Red Book (Penick with Shrake 1992)

That Same Day Over Lunch

Hank thought about the comment Jorge made about his putting. After the initial irritation, he thought he saw the point. We remember our once-in-a-lifetime shots. Sometimes they just happen, but that doesn't mean we should plan on hitting a career shot every time.

Jorge's discussion about the IEE strategy started the wheels turning in his head. He wondered why he had not heard of this before. He had always discounted Six Sigma as just another quality-improvement program, mostly because of the 3.4 DPMO discussions and Lean was to reduce waste. Whether he was right or not did not really matter. This afternoon's IEE discussion got him thinking otherwise.

Hank was frustrated that he had not tried earlier to understand IEE better when Jorge first mentioned it. The opportunities seemed endless. The idea of improving the enterprise measurement system and the way people do their jobs excited him. As he waited at the table for Jorge, he was anxious to learn more. Jorge certainly seemed to be doing well with it so far. He'd find out more details over lunch.

***

Jorge found Hank at a table by a window with a beautiful view of the golf course.

"What took you so long? Did you three-putt?" Hank teased him from across the room. "Tell me the details about how IEE works. I remember you told us about the training and the need to set up an infrastructure. What did that entail?"

Jorge responded, "After the one-week workout that I described previously, we established an Enterprise Process Management or EPM function as part of our value chain. This function was responsible for ensuring the refinement and execution of the E-DMAIC system that we roughed out in our one-week workout. As part of this EPM function, we established a steering committee

> After our one-week workout that I described previously, we established an Enterprise Process Management or EPM function as part of our value chain. This function was responsible for ensuring the refinement and execution of the E-DMAIC system that we roughed out in our one week workout.

which selected the champions and black belts. As we continue to roll out our IEE business strategy, we are learning that we will need to add green belts, which are part-time black belts, to help implement projects."

Hank nodded and asked, "What about project execution? How is this any different from the plan-do-check-act approach? You know, the one that Deming, the quality guru, wrote about."

"It's similar," commented Jorge. "Lean Six Sigma applies define-measure-analyze-improve-control to projects." This DMAIC methodology follows the same pattern as plan-do-check-act; however, each phase relates to the type of information you would be gathering during that phase. In IEE, we are using the P-DMAIC roadmap extension to guide us through each project execution phase. We follow the roadmap to help us understand, analyze, and then solve problems in our processes."

Lunch arrived and, as always, Jorge was amazed at how much food Hank could consume. "Where do you put all that food?" he asked incredulously. "If I ate as much as you do, I'd be over 300 pounds in no time!"

"The key, my friend, is exercise," Hank replied, "I run for an hour four mornings a week and lift weights the three other mornings. If you think about it, with 15 useful hours in a day, that's only about 6.7% of my week. For so little effort, I receive a lot of benefits. I can still beat the boys in basketball, and I seem to have more energy. Laura and I have even been swing dancing on Saturday nights, which keeps the romance alive."

Jorge thought for a moment about Laura. She was the first woman whom Hank had dated more than a few times after his divorce. They were good for each other, and Jorge figured that their romance was pretty healthy even without the dancing.

"You know, I've tried to stick with a daily exercise regimen, but I just can't seem to stay committed," lamented Jorge.

"Consistency is the key; you have to keep at it," urged Hank.

"That's funny," Jorge laughed. "Our IEE workshops are teaching the same basic ideas: reduce variation and stick to the roadmap."

"So, speaking of consistency, do you think I should create a histogram for both distance and direction for all my clubs?" asked Hank, thinking about the consistency and reduced variation arguments.

"Actually," Jorge said, "you probably already have. For example, I would estimate that your 160-yard 7 iron has a standard deviation of five or six yards. With these estimates you should plan accordingly. Don't depend upon hitting your personal best shot, or even your average shot, when picking your club."

***

After Hank devoured his large lunch, the conversation turned back to IEE. "So, you were talking about creating an IEE infrastructure," prompted Hank.

Jorge replied, "Creating a successful infrastructure that does more than simply hunt for projects is part of the define phase in the E-DMAIC roadmap. Managers need to develop a clear high-level view of their business so they can identify what areas provide the greatest opportunity for improvement. This is where the satellite-level metric strategy that I told you about comes in. Having no calendar boundaries in this methodology provides a system perspective.

> Creating a successful infrastructure that does more than simply hunt for projects is part of the define phase in the E-DMAIC roadmap.

"The Enron problem and other similar management-style problems would not have occurred if a no-nonsense governing system was in place. This system would have had a 30,000-foot-level metrics with a value chain that documented processes, and a system which faced waste and business improvement issues head-on.

"We found that the IEE workout really helped us get off to a good start. This event was similar in spirit to a Kaizen Event. It was also very helpful that our deployment consultant came to our facility every month to not only provide coaching for projects but also E-DMAIC implementation coaching. This helped create a system for both current and on-going project selection that was based on analysis, not somebody's opinion. There are critical parameters that you look for in initial projects in order to help assure success."

> We found that the IEE workout really helped us get off to a good start. This event was similar in spirit to a Kaizen event. It was also very helpful that our deployment partner came to our facility every month to not only provide coaching for projects but also E-DMAIC implementation coaching.

Jorge wrote the following project parameters on a napkin for Hank. (see Table 7.1):

Table 7.1: Project parameters.

- Project is important to the business' success and in alignment with business goals.
- Project will have a visible impact.
- Project is properly scoped so that the team does not become overwhelmed
- Project should be completed within six months (longer projects can be tackled later after Black Belts have gained more experience)
- Data is available to support the project

"Projects should be linked to the time-related value chain business metrics that can be used to impact how the business is doing. Using the right metrics lets you quantify the impact of projects on the business," Jorge explained.

"My wife and I were at a charity benefit last night," Jorge continued. "Lean Six Sigma was mentioned at our table, and it turned out that many of those we talked to were from companies that are implementing Lean Six Sigma. As you might expect, it became obvious during our discussions that companies were experiencing different amounts of success with Lean Six Sigma. Some companies have not had the kind of executive support from their CEO that we are experiencing and it seems that they've been less successful. For these situations, I cannot help but think that they could benefit from an IEE structure. I would suspect that in these organizations focus is given to meeting the month's numbers instead of creating a no-nonsense measurement and improvement system that orchestrates everyone's activities. I'm glad Janet, our CEO, is supporting the implementation and using the tools.

"Also, it was obvious that some of these companies weren't asking the right questions or using the best metrics, and their results suffered. For example, some companies were spending a lot of resources counting defects. They were trying to create a defect metric they could use for their entire company. They wanted to calculate an overall sigma quality level in every area of their business. Using this metric, an organization with a defect rate of 3.4 parts per million opportunities is said to be operating at a Six Sigma quality level. A three sigma quality level is about 67,000 ppm. A four sigma quality level is about 6000 ppm while a five sigma quality level is about 250 ppm.

"Some companies try to use this metric as a primary driver for their Lean Six Sigma implementation, and, while it sounds like a utopian metric, it has major problems. To use it, you have to define opportunities for failure for all activities within your company. This is not only a huge undertaking but also there can be discrepancies on how things are counted. Take your business, for example. What would you consider to be an opportunity for a defect on one of your printed circuit boards?"

Hank thought for a minute and answered, "When manufacturing circuit boards, we could have material problems, assembly problems, handling damage, ..."

Jorge interrupted, "Yeah, but what are the specific opportunities for defects? For example, what type of material problems?"

"Unfortunately, there are many. You could have components that are out of tolerance or broken. You could also have a cracked board. And then there are the assembly problems such as solder bridging, unsoldered joints, reversed parts, missing parts, even wrong parts."

Jorge replied, "From what I've learned in training, there's a standard approach for this situation. You don't count every way a component can have a problem. Instead, each component is counted as one opportunity, with multiple defect types. With this method, the total number of opportunities is obtained by adding the number of components and solder joints."

Jorge continued, "Let's approximate the sigma quality level of your printed circuit board manufacturing lines. How many components would there be per board?"

Hank chewed his fingernail, took a minute to silently count, and responded, "I'd say 300 to 400 for the Mach II line."

"About how many solder connections would you have?"

"About 600 to 800," Hank responded.

"Okay, let's say the total number of solder joints and components is 1000. How many boards would you make in a typical week? And also, how many defects would you expect?" Jorge asked as he jotted the numbers down on the napkin under the list of project parameters.

"We've been running about 5000 a week and our yield is around 98%," Hank responded immediately.

"Your yield is running about 98%, but how many defects were really created? There could be more than one defect on a board. Also, there could be defects repaired but not counted against the yield. What would you guess defects would be if they were all counted?"

Hank wavered and finally responded, "Well, I'm not certain, but we once did an engineering study on that line, indicating 1250 defects per week. I believe that included all the uncounted touchups and reworks."

"Okay," Jorge said, working the numbers on a new napkin. "For one week you have 5000 boards and each board has 1000 opportunities for defects. That's 5,000,000 opportunities for defects per week. If you divide 1250 defects by 5,000,000, you would have a 250 DPMO rate, which is about a five sigma quality level."

Hank responded, "That's pretty good. With just a little effort I could be at a six sigma quality level!"

"Not so fast, sigma boy. For one thing, you are operating at a 250 DPMO rate or a five sigma quality level. The sigma quality-level metric is not linear. Each incremental improvement is harder than the one before. You would have to make significant process changes to operate at a 3.4 DPMO rate.

"Secondly, consider the average number of defects you have per board. You have 1250 defects for the 5000 boards you make per week That could be viewed as an average rework rate of 25%. Doesn't sound so good to me. Looks like you have what we learned in our training as 'hidden factory.' You're doing a lot of rework that is hidden and isn't showing up in your yield numbers. So, you can see how the sigma quality level metric and even the final yield number are sometimes deceiving," Jorge elaborated and paused to let Hank take it all in. His wheels were obviously spinning.

"Let's step back a second and ask yourself why you have these measures," Jorge spoke, breaking Hank's thought stream.

Hank responded, "We use them as part of our cost of operations. We want to see if we are improving or not. We also want to keep customers happy by delivering good products."

Jorge then replied, "Okay, let's talk costs. Shouldn't you be counting all reworks in your cost calculations? If you're only focusing on final yield numbers, you're missing the cost impact of all those reworks. In IEE terms, we refer to this as the cost of poor quality (COPQ) or the cost of doing nothing differently (CODND). This number paints a better picture of what's really happening in your operation. Rather than patting yourself on the back for having a 98% yield or quoting a five sigma quality level, you track the comprehensive DPMO rate over time and convert that to COPQ/CODND.

"By doing it this way, you have the true cost. In addition, details of the hidden factory defects can be compiled and used to determine where to focus improvements and subsequently reduce costs."

Hank sat silently with a perplexed frown. He folded up the two napkins carefully and placed them in his worn billfold. After a few minutes, Jorge grew uneasy with the silence, asking his friend if he had rambled too much.

"No, everything makes perfect sense. I'm just wondering how much 98% yield is actually costing the business. First thing on Monday, I'm going to have someone get me the numbers," Hank resolved.

Jorge added, "Well, you've got the idea, but there are a few more areas in which the sigma quality level can be deceiving. I'll give your brain a rest and explain those another time."

Hank beat Jorge to the bill when it arrived. Jorge protested that Hank had won on the last hole, but Hank just smiled and said that this was the most cost-effective business lunch he had ever had. It not only helped him fix his golf game, it had given him a new perspective on his attempts to improve his business. Jorge settled for a chance to buy Hank a beer in the bar.

Hank was hungry for more details, relentless in his search for ways to work more efficiently, and asked, "Jorge, you've talked a lot about training. What does that entail?"

"Technically, I didn't need to attend the black belt training. The four week-long sessions over four months really cut into my schedule, but I knew I could do a better job leading the implementation if I was familiar with the details.

"The first week's primary focus is on project definition and the measure phase of P-DMAIC. This is not uncommon within many Lean Six Sigma training sessions. However, the topics covered within these phases and how it is done can be quite different depending upon the training provider. Black belts are also given a high-level view of the E-DMAIC steps and how many tools of the P-DMAIC process are also applicable in E-DMAIC.

"In our training, the P-DMAIC measure phase had two components: creating baseline metrics and gathering the Wisdom of the Organization. During the week, we talked about obtaining the voice of the customer and the high-level metrics necessary to describe the outputs of the current process in a manner that leads to the right activities.

"One main component of week-one training is the creation of 30,000-foot-level control charts and process capability/performance metrics that I spoke of earlier. This type of charting is applicable not only to project tracking but also the reporting of value chain scorecard/dashboard metrics. Unlike red-yellow-green scorecards, this form of performance reporting can get companies out of the firefighting mode."

"You know, Jorge, I don't see any high-level type metrics in our Lean rollout. Don't get me wrong, Lean techniques are helping us make some gains, but we are not getting the high-level view of our operation. Now that I think of it, there has been a lot of confusion and debate over where to focus our efforts initially."

"Hank, you really should look into using these charts to help focus your Lean efforts. The other day, the woman next to me on my flight home was a Lean champion, similar to a Lean Six Sigma black belt. She told me that one of the first projects their Lean consultant had them do was reduce finished goods inventory to almost nothing. Predictably, as soon as their inventory went down, a big order came in. They were forced to spend a lot of money in overtime and expediting shipments.

"When I told her about how we're learning to use a satellite-level metric view strategy for our various processes, manufacturing as well as transactional, she told me that they would never have chosen some of their projects if they had considered this type of high-level view of their operations.

"Then we talked about how the project might have gone if they had followed the P-DMAIC roadmap I was taught in training. We sketched a rough plan out for her which considered the demand pattern and cycle time of the system and then determined what the finished goods inventory level should have been."

"If you saved all the napkins from all of our IEE discussions, you could give your own training class," Hank acknowledged with a smile. "So far, we've been focusing on improving our lead times. This may not be a completely fair statement, but, it seems after making some improvements, we generate defects faster now! What I am really interested in, after our talk, is how are we impacting the bottom line?"

"So, let's talk about your Mach II product line," Jorge said. "What do you think is the biggest problem area?"

Hank said, "We're having problems with both defects and lead times."

Jorge quickly interjected, "What about WIP?"

Hank responded, "Our initial thoughts were WIP was not as big of a problem as defects and lead times; however, we might change our mind if we tracked this metric using your 30,000-foot-level metric strategy."

"Which is costing you the most money? Don't forget customer dissatisfaction costs money, too."

Hank responded, "Based on previous conversations, I think that defects are our biggest problem. I don't think that our on-time delivery record is really that bad. However, in one of our team meetings, I discovered that our lead times are apparently a lot longer than our competition. Some people in my organization think that our lengthy lead times could be causing us to lose a lot of new-customer orders."

Jorge pulled a stack of napkins from the bar, rolled up his sleeves, and with a proud smile, said, "Okay, for now let's consider customer defective rate as your primary metric with lead time, WIP, and defect rate as secondary metrics. I have included defect rate tracking since this metric could expose an ugly internal rework program that can be very costly and have a major impact on lead time. When doing this, we will be tracking all four metrics at the 30,000-foot-level. In the project, we want the 30,000-foot-level to shift to a new, improved level of predictability. We surely don't want the other metrics to degrade; however, we might be able to get them to improve, also.

"So let's start outlining a P-DMAIC project for you to reduce defects in your Mach II product line." Jorge was eager to strategize, but his mechanical pencil was out of lead. He bummed a pen from the bartender, then asked, "How do you currently address defects in production?"

"Well," Hank responded, "We set a criterion for the number of allowable defective units per day. When we exceed those targets, we take corrective action."

"This is not unlike Zack's red-yellow-green scorecards. Does your production process exceed this criterion often?" Jorge inquired.

"Unfortunately, yes," Hank responded.

Jorge responded, "I would bet that if you tracked these defects on a 30,000-foot-level control chart, you'd find you're doing a lot work and nothing is improving. That is, you are doing a lot of firefighting. In class, the instructor would say that you are attacking common-cause variability as though it were special cause. When you're firefighting, you're not improving the process and could even make it worse. If you send me some numbers, I'll look at them and make some suggestions.

"Before I forget, I need to have these numbers in a particular format. To determine this format I need to ask a few questions. Do you expect to get differences between days of the week?"

After a few seconds of thought, Hank replied, "Yes, I think that shift differences or daily raw material lots could affect part quality."

"If you don't think that there will be differences between weeks of the month, we will subgroup by week."

Hank response was, "I cannot think of any reason why defective rates should differ by week of a month."

"Okay, what I would like to see is a spreadsheet where each row summarizes data from one week. Let me show you what I am looking for (see Table 7.2)."

"As you can see in this spreadsheet, I want data for tracking both your primary and secondary metrics. If you have the lead times for all units that would be great. If not, I would like for you to list five randomly selected lead times from each week. I would also like to receive as much historical data as possible. If you can

Table 7.2: Data collection sheet

Week start date	Number units produced	Number of defectives	Number of defects	WIP	Lead time random unit #1	Lead time random unit #2	Lead time random unit #3	Lead time random unit #4	Lead time random unit #5

list data for ten years, do it. Just e-mail the spreadsheet to me whenever you have it done."

After taking a few minutes to contemplate the request, Hank said, "It will take some effort, but I think that I can get this put together for you. Why not just look at the data from the last year and make some comparisons."

"If you made that statement in our class, the instructor would get on his soap box stating something to the effect that in IEE our efforts are focusing on understanding the process and the process has no recollection of calendar boundaries. If something changed in July and it is now December of the following year, making annual comparisons would not be fair since the change impact would be spread across two years. We will take note of both positive and negative shifts whenever they occur and report it accordingly.

"If your process experiences only common-cause variability, we would need to examine your data collectively to determine the capability of your process. If the results are not satisfactory, you'll need to work on the overall process. This is called a key process output variable or KPOV."

> If your process experiences only common cause variability, we would need to examine your data collectively to determine the capability of your process. If the results are not satisfactory, you'll need to work on the overall process.

"Geeze," Hank said pensively. "Yesterday I really laid into the plant manager at our San Francisco facility for not meeting his monthly targets. I then asked the manager to determine what happened during the last measurement period, forcing him into the firefighting mode, I'm sure, which will probably lead to more inefficient actions."

Hank whacked himself playfully on the forehead. "I asked the wrong question. I bet a lot of my managers fire-fight events that stem from common-cause variability. We should be focusing on data over a longer period of time, to get a picture of the process, and then analyze what we need to do differently to improve."

"Exactly," Jorge responded, excited that his paper napkin class was beginning to sink into Hank's thinking.

Hank, inspired that things were beginning to make sense, continued, "The implications of this metric could be huge. We could apply this approach to many other areas of the business, including sales and service. Taking a high-level view of our key processes over time could help us reduce the amount of daily firefighting, creating a view of our entire organization as a system. Then, we could proactively drill down and create P-DMAIC projects that really impact the bottom line."

After shoveling a handful of pretzels into his mouth and washing it down with ice water, Hank asked, "Did you read the *Fifth Discipline* by Peter Senge (Senge 1990)?"

Jorge hadn't, so Hank explained, "He talks about a learning organization. If implemented wisely, we can use these metrics and other tools within IEE to help our organization become a learning organization. We would become curious about our processes, embrace change, and gain confidence with each successful improvement. This could transform our organization and increase growth, which is really what is important to our shareholders."

> If implemented wisely, we can use these metrics and other tools within IEE to help our organization become a learning organization.

Jorge stole the pretzel bowl away from Hank before Hank devoured them all. Now he was starving. He looked down at his watch, surprised to find that it was already time for dinner. Time just flew whenever he started talking about IEE and its benefits. Maybe he should consider becoming a full-time instructor.

***

As the sun began to set on the golf course, Jorge and Hank decided to stay and have dinner on the patio of the clubhouse, enjoying the sunset and finishing their discussion.

Once they had ordered, Jorge continued, "Our instructor stressed that organizations achieving success learn to apply the most appropriate tool or measure for each process. There is no one-size-fits-all metric or tool appropriate for all processes."

"Hmmm ... Sort of like learning that changing to a 3 iron off the tee is not the answer for everyone. You are saying that IEE offers some useful metrics that could be beneficial to a particular process but not necessarily to all processes," Hank reiterated.

"As I mentioned earlier, DPMO is a metric that some organizations try to force onto every process, but it's not always easy to describe what an opportunity is for every process." Jorge fished around for something to sketch on, but the napkins were cloth, causing them both to chuckle.

Improvising, Jorge pulled a receipt from his billfold and illustrated an example for defects on a piece of sheet metal. A natural teacher, as he drew he lectured, "You could describe a defect opportunity as one square inch, one square foot, or one square millimeter. You can see the confusion that could arise with multiple definitions for opportunities. In transactional processes, this practice gets even crazier. However, as we talked about before, DPMO does have its uses."

Hank hungrily picked up the receipt, folded it carefully, and placed it in his billfold next to the napkins from lunch, as Jorge continued, "Another Six Sigma metric, which may or may not be useful, is rolled throughput yield (RTY). This metric can be useful to describe the hidden factory we talked about earlier. It is calculated by multiplying together the yields for each step of the process. This can highlight the amount of rework within a process and where it is occurring. However, this metric can require a lot of work to generate and is not appropriate for all situations."

The waiter brought their dinners and they each ordered a beer with their meal, which was inspired by Jorge's recent trip to Ireland with Sandra. They took a break from their informal class and devoured the battered deep-fried fish and salty fries. Hank shared the highlights of their week-long bicycling tour, mostly detailing the pubs and the people of Ireland.

After dinner, the waiter delivered coffee Hank had requested. Jorge continued his lecture but warned Hank that he would have to wrap things up soon and get home.

"So, after deciding a primary 30,000-foot-level metric, you then assess whether your process is in control and has the capability to deliver a desirable output. If the process is not capable of meeting customer requirements, you would then tap the Wisdom of the Organization via people who know the process intimately. The end goal is to solicit improvement ideas using brainstorming tools such as cause-and-effect diagrams."

Hank, intrigued but confused, asked, "Can you give me an actual example?"

Jorge said, "I think that we have graduated from napkins. I have some papers in the car that I can use to explain the concepts. Give me a couple minutes to get them."

As Jorge was leaving Hank's wheels started turning on how his organization could benefit from the techniques that Jorge was using.

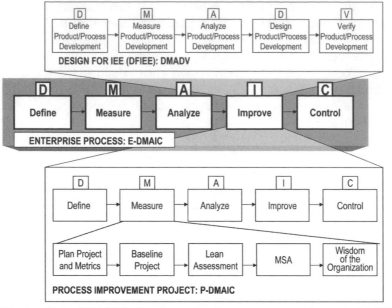

Figure 7.1: IEE high-level enterprise process roadmap with DMAIC
process improvement and DMADV
(define-measure-analyze-design-verify) design project roadmaps
(MSA = measurement systems analysis).

Upon his return Jorge opened a folder and said, "This is the
roadmap that we are following. Let's start with the E-DMAIC portion of this overall IEE roadmap (see Figure 7.1).

"Hank, a part of the E-DMAIC define and measure phases is
the value chain with its scorecard/dashboard metrics. Here is a
generic example that was presented in our training workshop (See
Figure 7.2). The financial metrics shown for the last step is the
satellite-level metrics. All other metrics are considered 30,000-
foot-level metrics. Satellite-level and 30,000-foot-level metric
reporting does not have calendar boundaries. What I mean
by that is if our charting indicates that there has not been a
response change in ten years our response will reflect ten years
of information. Note how this approach is quite different from
simply reporting annual or quarterly statements, which can
drive the wrong behaviors near the end of the reporting time
period when we give focus to what can be done so we meet our
numbers."

"Jorge, that sure is different," Hank interjected. "I can see how
this could dramatically change our culture for the better. Currently
we are driving people to some arbitrary improvement goal that is

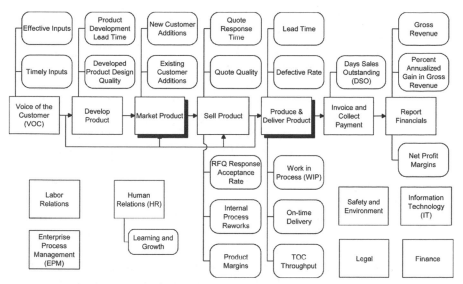

Figure 7.2: Value chain with scorecard/dashboard metrics. Shaded areas designate processes that have sub-process drill downs.

annually set. I'll bet if we go back and look at the numbers we would find that no real long-lasting improvements have been made."

> I can see how this could dramatically change our culture for the better. Currently we are driving people to some arbitrary improvement goal that is annually set. I'll bet if we go back and look at the numbers we would find that no real long-lasting improvements have been made.

"Hank, what you describe is not that uncommon in organizations. What I am suggesting is a no-nonsense approach for reporting metrics. Accountability would be established through the value chain for each metric. If the organizational strategy indicates that a particular metric is to be improved to meet organizational financial goals, the person who is accountable for the metric is responsible for making the process change to accomplish it. For companies, like ours, that have performance plans, this would be an item that should be included. These 30,000-foot-level metric goals are not to be bound by calendar years. For example, we might state that a 30,000-foot-level metric should be improved in six months, which is the first week of September. To achieve this goal, we would need to see a sustained statistical significant improvement shift in the 30,000-foot-level metric by the first week of September."

"Hank interrupted, "Jorge, you made a statement about strategy that caught my attention. It seems like everything we do in our company is driven from strategies. A couple years ago a strategy was created to outsource. We have been focusing our efforts to meet that strategy; however, I am not confident that this is the best strategy for the business. In addition, since that time we have had other strategies come and go. Some of them are also not very specific. They are not much different from what Zack showed us on a previous outing. In addition, I am not sure that we are coming up with the right strategies for the whole business to follow. It sounds like your IEE system has a different approach for strategy creation."

"You are right, Hank," Jorge replied. Let me describe the overall process for this. In the E-DMAIC analyze phase we do what the name implies. We structurally analyze the enterprise data from an overall process improvement perspective to determine where our efforts should focus in order to meet our goals. This analysis leads to the data-driven enterprise improvement plan or EIP creation."

Jorge then turns the page in his folder, "See how this EIP graphic drills down from organizational goals through the building of strategies to specific projects (see Figure 7.3)."

Jorge pointed to the EIP chart and said, "See how this one EIP drilled down to lead to a DSO project that has a goal to reduce mean DSO by three days in seven months? This project will illustrate some of the concepts that we have been talking about. It's a transactional project dealing with days sales outstanding or DSO. This is a value chain metric that we agreed needed to improve in order to meet our financial goals. DSO is typically the average number of days it takes to collect revenue after a sale has been made. For purposes of this study we defined it as the number of days before or after the due date that a payment is received.

"To create this metric, consider that we randomly select one invoice daily. We could select more, however, I want to start with a simple illustration.

"First we defined DSO as when a payment was received relative to the due date. If it was a day early, we would record a -1 for the KPOV, in this case, DSO. If it was a day late, we would record a $+1$ for the KPOV. Then, we control chart DSO at the 30,000-foot-level."

Jorge pointed to a DSO control chart (see Figure 7.4) and said, "Control charts have an upper control limit or UCL. They also have a lower control limit or LCL. The data and its variability determine these limits. That is, what you desire or specification

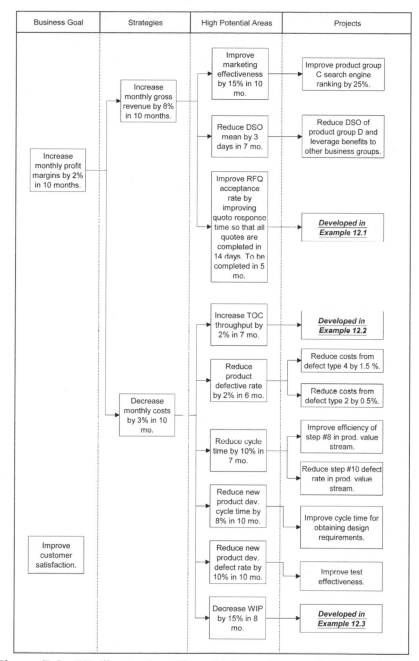

Figure 7.3: EIP illustration. Three Volume 2 examples are referred to in this figure as potential improvement projects. For example, *Developed in Example 12.1* refers to chapter (i.e., 12) and example number (i.e., 1) in Volume 2 of this series.

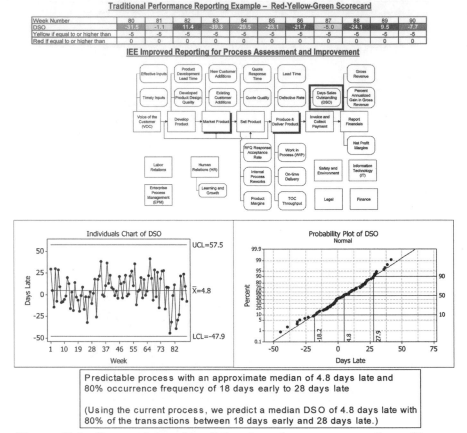

Traditional Performance Reporting Example – Red-Yellow-Green Scorecard

Week Number	80	81	82	83	84	85	86	87	88	89	90
DSO	-31.5	-1.1	11.4	-39.3	-29.5	-23.1	-21.7	-5.0	-24.1	9.5	-7.7
Yellow if equal to or higher than	-5	-5	-5	-5	-5	-5	-5	-5	-5	-5	-5
Red if equal to or higher than	0	0	0	0	0	0	0	0	0	0	0

IEE Improved Reporting for Process Assessment and Improvement

Predictable process with an approximate median of 4.8 days late and 80% occurrence frequency of 18 days early to 28 days late

(Using the current process, we predict a median DSO of 4.8 days late with 80% of the transactions between 18 days early and 28 days late.)

Figure 7.4: Comparison of traditional performance reporting with an IEE value chain 30,000-foot-level DSO performance scorecard/dashboard report. The traditional performance reporting example contains the most recent eleven data points.

limits have no affect on these calculated limits. This plot of the control chart is the first stage of the process talking to us."

Jorge then selected a napkin and wrote two equations. "Since you are an engineer, I will show an equation for calculating our control chart limits," he said.

$$\text{LCL} = \bar{x} - 2.66\overline{MR} \qquad \text{UCL} = \bar{x} + 2.66\overline{MR}$$

"As you can see LCL and UCL are determined from the overall mean or x-bar and the mean moving range or $\overline{MR}$. In this equation, moving range is the amount of change between two adjacent data points."

Hank asked, "Why the 2.66 factor?"

"I knew you were going to ask that. If you recall from one of your university statistics classes, standard deviation is a measure of variability. For a normal distribution, three standard deviations from the mean captured 99.73% of the population. The 2.66 $\overline{MR}$ multiple is simply three times the sampling standard deviation. That is, if the process is stable, we expect a random scatter within these limits. If this occurs, we can say that the process is predictable.

"For predictable processes, we can use historical data to make a prediction for the future. With this prediction, we are making the presumption that something different does not occur in the process which either positively or negatively impacts the process response.

"If there is a specification limit, we would then make a statement relative to the percentage of nonconformity that we expect in the future. If there is no specification limit, we can then make a best estimate median statement and 80% frequency of occurrence. These statements quantify how the process is doing relative to voicing customer needs."

Jorge then pointed again to the sheet of paper saying, "See how this example DSO report illustrates a 30,000-foot-level metric statement in terms that everyone can understand: predictable process with an approximate median of 4.8 days late, and 80% occurrence frequency of 18 days early to 28 days late. Some people new to IEE might initially prefer a statement like: using the current process, we predict a median DSO of 4.8 days late with 80% of the transactions between 18 days early and 28 days late.

"See how this figure also compares an IEE presentation to a red-yellow-green scorecard report out. Note how the red colored signals, which were determined from business goals, can be triggering the firefighting of common-cause variability issues as though they were a special cause."

Hank responded, "Wow! Think about it! The setting of goals throughout the organization through red-yellow-green scorecards with no fundamental process improvement plans for each of these metrics can lead to a huge amount of firefighting. This can eat up a tremendous amount of resource! I would think that we should be using analytics to better figure out where we should be focusing our metrics improvement efforts relative to overall business needs."

Jorge responded, "Right on! Another thing that we could do to help with that selection process is determine the business cost impact from the metrics. This report would reflect a calculation for the metric that we discussed earlier; that is, the cost of doing nothing differently or CODND."

"With the IEE approach, we have examined data over a relatively long period of time to determine if the process is predictable. When the process is shown to be predictable, the next question is, 'How are we doing relative to the needs of our customers?' We then used process capability/performance metric techniques to describe this. As an alternative, we could also have estimated from the probability plot the percentage of times we failed to meet customer needs. To determine this value, we would initiate from the x-axis and move up the plot and then over to the y-axis," Jorge spoke easily as he used a pen to point out this additional probability plot usage.

After finishing his drawing, Jorge continued, "We also calculated the cost of not receiving payment by the due date. An interesting part of this project is that we learned to convert DSO from a pass-fail attribute response to a numeric response. The advantage of using a numeric response is that if we set up a criterion of 60 days, a payment of 61 days is not weighted the same as a payment of 120 days.

"A high-level finance manager would be the owner of this value chain metric. From the EIP, we have a specific SMART goal for this metric. The finance manager would surely need help determining what to do to improve their processes so that DSO decreases. This is a pull for project creation that management has a burning-platform need for initiation and completion."

Hank interjected, "You know, what you just described is a strategy that addresses the process x in a relationship $Y=f(x)$. This is different from what Enron did and others are doing. They are focusing or even adjusting the financials at the Y level. What they are missing is that the only true long-lasting improvement in a Y response is through improvements in the x or process steps that impact Y."

You know what you just described is a strategy that addresses the process x in a relationship $Y=f(x)$. This is different that what Enron did and others are doing. They are focusing or even adjusting the financials at the Y level. What they are missing is that the only true long-lasting improvement in a Y response is through improvements in the x or process steps that impact Y.

Jorge exclaimed, "Boy, you are picking up on this quickly! That is exactly what was described in our workshops."

Hank then responded, "The term SMART goal that you referenced seems familiar but I cannot remember the details."

Jorge said, "Not everyone uses the same letter descriptors for SMART. My training suggested that goals should be set so that they are specific, measurable, actionable, relevant and time based."

Jorge then continued, "It is important to highlight that the DSO metric is part of the organization's overall value chain and has a tracking format that assesses process performance over time. That is, we did not all of a sudden decide to create a metric and put the metric into a format for an improvement project, which is often done in Lean Six Sigma projects.

"For the finance manager to meet this metric goal, the need to solicit the aid of a black belt or green belt to head up the process improvement project is imperative. In the project, a Wisdom-of-the-Organization P-DMAIC step would then help capture where your initial focus should be when looking for process improvement opportunities. This early assessment can save a lot of time and money in that resources are not spent collecting data in areas that have a small likelihood for being beneficial to the project. This activity is not much different than a murder mystery where clues are collected to determine '*who done it*', Jorge explained with satisfaction.

The light bulb in Hank's head flashed on, and he commented, "You know, something you said earlier just hit me. Airlines should do the same form of metric reporting that you described earlier. If a flight leaves within 15 minutes of scheduled departure, it's considered on time. This means a flight that is three hours late is no more late than one that is 16 minutes late. From a customer point of view, that doesn't make sense."

Jorge said, "You're right. This form of attribute response reporting reemphasizes that we need to have metrics that encourage the right activities throughout the organization on a continuous basis. If a flight is 16 minutes late, why should the crew rush since they have already been given a failure check mark for being late for that particular flight departure?"

Hank leaned back a moment and smiled, "And it's sort of like one of my putts that misses the hole by a few inches, compared to one that misses by a few feet. They are both defects, but the first one only costs me one stroke, while the second may cost more."

The golf comment made Jorge think of Wayne and Zack. "One of the defects that caused Zack to miss today's game was transaction errors. This is another type of problem that could be a part of the value chain and tracked as a 30,000-foot-level metric, which, like other metrics would have an owner. If this metric level is unsatisfactory from an enterprise viewpoint, there would then be a pull for creating a P-DMAIC project that a team would tackle.

"I wonder how Zack is addressing this transactional error problem with the balanced scorecard system. I would suspect that the balanced scorecard deployment does not suggest the creation of a value chain with 30,000-foot-level reported metrics. Traditional deployments of the balanced scorecard system do not formally have the completed measurement and improvement structure of E-DMAIC. That is, even though the balanced scorecard system might identify a problem, improvement efforts to the system don't seem to have the benefit of describing the how-to's of making improvements at the process level. Also, the benefits of 30,000-foot-level metric reporting do not seem to be prevalent in the balanced scorecard systems that I have encountered."

Jorge continued, "The scope of this as an IEE project might be to improve the transaction entry process in order to reduce the number of transaction errors at a single office. For this situation, the number of transaction errors would be the KPOV. Remember that the KPOV is important because it can tell you whether the customer is going to be satisfied. Notice, however, that this measurement comes too late in the process to avoid waste or an unsatisfied customer."

Hank handed him another napkin as Jorge calculated Zack's example.

"So, in Zack's case, if there are 2.5 transaction errors per 1000 in one month, and 4.8 per 1000 in the next, how do you know if the transaction entry process has changed for the worse?" Jorge asked.

"What kind of question is that? Of course it's getting worse," Hank responded without thinking.

"It seems like it is getting worse, but you can't really tell until you compare it to the normal range of the process. In the class, 30,000-foot-level control charts established the range of common-cause variability. If a 30,000-foot-level control chart had limits of 1.75 to 6.0 errors per 1000 transactions, then there is no evidence to indicate that the process has changed for the months with 2.5 and 4.8 errors per 1000 transactions," Jorge turned teacher again. "The 30,000-foot-level control chart is useful to baseline our process. A baseline is important here because it answers questions about when process changes occur."

Hank thought about improving his golf game again. "So I should keep 30,000-foot-level control charts on my golf scores, maybe even the number of fairways and greens hit, and number of putts per round just so I'll know when I need to practice a particular part of my game?"

Jorge nodded and said, "Exactly. And you could also use them to see if your practice was working."

Shifting gears, he continued, "Up until now we've been talking about the measure phase. The next step of the DMAIC process is the analyze phase. The key to solving problems is to find what step within the process is driving the KPOVs. Key process input variables or KPIVs influence the KPOVs. In Zack's case, the KPIVs may be the number of transactions a clerk has to handle hourly or the method of entering transactions into the computer. So the measure phase is focused on developing a baseline for the KPOVs and collecting Wisdom of the Organization on what the KPIVs might be. To do this, we would use tools such as cause-and-effect diagrams, cause-and-effect matrices, and failure mode and effects analyses, or FMEA.

"Then, in the analyze phase, we test hypothesized cause-and-effect relationships to see if there is statistical significance. Areas found significant can lead us to new insights about where we should focus our improvement efforts."

Hank was really excited. He saw the possibilities of this methodology. This would allow him to restructure the implementation of his Lean program to focus on bottom-line issues. He could use this approach to attack the loss of market share! After all, that was a KPOV. Surely there had to be some KPIVs that he could use to improve market share.

The waiter interrupted Jorge's class and placed the bill on the table. Hank quickly grabbed it again. "I'll get this one, Jorge; it is the least I can do for the time you have spent with me today. I know you have a lot of other things going on right now, plus I need room in my wallet for the rest of the class," Hank stated gratefully.

"Thank you, Hank, but it has really been my pleasure. Let's wrap this class up and we will talk more on another day, probably the next golf outing. Since you are now an advanced student, you can help me inform the others," Jorge said jokingly.

8

Turning Point

Don't Relax

If you try real hard to relax, you will become either very tense or else so limp you might fall over...

... I prefer to put it this way: Be at ease. If you feel at ease, you are relaxed—but ready.

Harvey Penick's Little Red Book (Penick with Shrake 1992)

September

A few days before their September golf date, Jorge called Hank. "I realized that I had not talked to you about the voice of the customer. This is critical to everything else you do with IEE. Unless you understand what the customers want or need, you can't tell how they think you're doing. Haven't you been frustrated at times about poor service? Could it be that the provider doesn't know what you want?"

Hank responded, "I sure have. For example, they keep putting these surveys on the golf carts asking for our evaluation of the golf course. It sure seems like they ask the wrong questions. At the bottom I sometimes write my comments, but nothing changes. I think that it's not too much to ask that they offer a decaffeinated soft drink on the refreshment golf cart. I have mentioned it several times on the form as well as to the person driving the cart."

"Exactly," Jorge responded. "What good are surveys if nobody reads them or ever takes action? Important feedback goes to some front-line employee and never gets to someone who can make a difference. Within IEE, we want to create processes that give us

81

the true voice of the customer at the value chain level and use it to help drive our internal improvements."

> What good are surveys if nobody reads them or ever takes action? Important feedback goes to some front-line employee and never gets to someone who can make a difference. Within IEE, we want to create processes that give us the true voice of the customer at the value chain level and use it to help drive our internal improvements.

***

Hank was excited to be on his way to the golf course to meet the guys. He had met with Jorge's IEE provider, and things were progressing well. His team had worked with Jorge's provider during a week-long workout at their facility. During this week they created their organizational value chain and 30,000-foot-level metrics. In addition, during the week they also roughed out a basic E-DMAIC infrastructure. They revisited their strategic plan and were working on overhauling it.

They had also assigned the job of understanding customer needs to some key employees in the marketing department. Yesterday, their EIP (see Figure 7.3 EIP example) identified projects in new product development, warehousing, and shipping. But Hank was most excited about the specific project of which he was champion: reducing manufacturing cycle time for their Mach II product line. He was accountable for this metric in their value chain. He practically had the entire project on Jorge's paper napkins completed, and it tied in nicely with his company's current Lean activities.

The management team could see how their Lean philosophy and tools fitted nicely into both the E-DMAIC and P-DMAIC roadmap. They could see how both roadmaps effectively utilized the Lean and Six Sigma tools.

In his almost ten years with Hi-Tech, this was the first time Hank had seen the connection between the overall business goals, strategies, and planned improvement projects. He felt more confident now than when they were implementing Lean without the IEE structure. The estimated savings were calculated in the millions the first year, which would more than pay for the training and consulting investments.

***

As Hank pulled into the parking lot, he saw the others congregated around Jorge's SUV. Jorge was sitting on the back bumper with the hatch open, changing shoes.

"Good morning," Hank called out to the group as he lifted his bag from the trunk of his red convertible.

Jorge and Wayne replied, but Zack seemed preoccupied. Zack had shown up to play golf, but he was having a tough time concentrating. The CEO at Z-Credit Financial had reorganized the company and moved him to VP of operations for a smaller firm they had recently purchased. Zack was especially upset that the CEO had brought in his latest whiz kid to turn things around within Zack's former group. It had all happened over two weeks before, but Zack was still upset and couldn't make sense of how things had gotten so bad.

"What's wrong, Zack?" Hank asked, not quite expecting the answer he received.

"We had a reorganization. They reassigned me to VP of operations for some little company we just bought. Technically, it was a lateral move, but it sure feels like a demotion. I think our CEO wasn't happy with my performance so he put me in this company that can't be screwed up any more than it already is. My replacement is a whiz kid from Harvard who used to report to me and is my son's age. I start my new job as soon as 'wonder boy' gets back from vacation in two weeks."

"I'm sorry to hear that, Zack," Jorge sympathized.

"This offers you a great opportunity to take a nothing company and turn it around," Wayne offered, in an attempt to lift Zack's spirits.

Zack responded, "How can I turn around a company that is in the dumps when I couldn't run a company that had a solid performance history? I tried to get things turned around through the balanced scorecard deployment. We spent a lot of time working to align and translate strategies into specific actions through the scorecards; however, I am not sure that our strategies are that great. Our strategy wording is often hard to get our minds around."

Hank was about to jump in to say that he agreed with the point he was making about strategies and tell him all the news about IEE, but before he could get started Jorge said, "Hey, let's play. We can talk about this later. Right now, I'm going to teach you guys a thing or two about golf."

Sensing Zack's distress, Jorge decided to change the game in an attempt to avoid a total meltdown. At the first tee, Jorge said,

"Let's change things today. Let's play a two-man scramble. Each player hits his shot, and then each team selects the best of their two shots and both partners play their next stroke from there. We can keep the same teams so that each side has a long-ball hitter and a short-game player. It should be fun for a change. The team with the lowest total score wins. Same bet?"

Everyone agreed, although no one's heart really seemed to be in it. They played four holes before anyone mentioned work, a course record. By that time, Zack really needed to vent and said, "I don't understand what happened. I was really working hard putting together the balanced scorecard system. However, I just had difficulty seeing improvements in the projects that were created. It seemed like everyone was going in a different direction."

Wayne commiserated, attempting to ease Zack's nerves, "You know, we've been having some success as well, but our Lean Six Sigma deployment hasn't been what I expected. We now have a whole Lean Six Sigma group that is to work with some of our management team in a steering committee role. It seems like there are always disagreements and misunderstandings. The Lean Six Sigma group doesn't seem to understand the pressure on the production managers to meet their schedules and quotas. In turn, the production managers are always complaining that the Lean Six Sigma projects shut their lines down to fix problems that don't really affect production. It seems like the only projects we're having success with are the cross-functional ones in which the process owner is truly championing the project."

"That's it!" cried Hank as he totally missed his tee shot, which went about 60 yards. But he didn't seem to mind the distraction or the bad shot. "That's one of the key differences between IEE and Lean Six Sigma. With IEE, the people responsible for the process are responsible for improving it. You can't achieve success with a separate group to fix problems. There is no buy-in. The 30,000-foot-level metric system is a no-nonsense approach from which goals can be set and monitored to see if these goals are achieved and maintained."

> With IEE, the people responsible for the process are responsible for improving it. You can't achieve success with a separate group to fix problems. There is no buy-in. The 30,000-foot-level metric systems is a no nonsense approach from which goals can be set and monitored to see if these goals are achieved and maintained.

"When did you become an expert on IEE?" probed Wayne.

"I wasn't, until last month," Hank said sarcastically while pointing his driver at Wayne and Zack, "When you two were too busy working to join us. Jorge explained IEE to me, and a light went on. You boys missed an interesting discussion."

Wayne asked, "Jorge must have said something really good to get you off the Lean bandwagon. What did he say?"

"I'll lay it out for you at lunch," Hank responded. "I still have all my notes and Jorge sent me copies of the other information that he talked about."

Out on the fairway, Hank and Jorge made the easy decision to play Jorge's drive. It was a typical Jorge shot of modest length and a slight fade. But it was on the fairway, and the green was reachable. It was far better than Hank's distracted effort. Hank commented, "I guess that was really an outlier on my driver control chart." Jorge agreed that there probably was a real special cause this time: the distraction during his swing. From their position on the fairway, Jorge hit a decent fairway wood to the front edge of the green, and then Hank hit a magnificent 4 iron to the center of the green. "This team stuff has its benefits in a scramble," both thought as they moved on.

Meanwhile, Wayne hit another typical drive, long and straight in the middle of the fairway, making Zack's wild hook of no consequence. Hank thought briefly, "My maximum distance is better than Wayne's, but his distance and directional variation are less than half of mine. I should benchmark his driving process."

Wayne and Zack both hit their second shots, with short irons, from where Wayne's drive had landed. When they reached the green, they were farther away and putted first. Zack looked over the 18-footer, and putted. Zack saw the break and his read was perfect, but his stroke was a bit strong. His ball rimmed out of the cup and spun about two feet past it.

"Good read, partner—good putt," said Wayne. He had been standing directly behind Zack on line with the hole during his putt. He had not seen the subtle break at the end of the putt, but, armed with knowledge, he stepped up and sweetly stroked the 18-footer into the back of the cup.

"Great putt," exclaimed Zack. "Way to go, partner."

"It was easy once you showed me the line," said Wayne. "How did you know it would break at the end like that?"

Zack was confused, "What do you mean? I just looked at it and could see the break at the end. Also, I could see the grain was against us, so it would be a little slower and break a bit more. All I did was look at it. That's all I ever do."

"Me too," said Wayne, "But I certainly didn't see that little break or the grain." Suddenly it struck him. "You know, I've been having some trouble finding my ball when it is not on the fairway, too. Karen is right! Maybe I do need to get my eyes checked."

Hank chimed in, "You know, they say that tiger was seeing the breaks in the green better after he got that laser eye surgery. It was right before he started that incredible run of victories. I think they can even make corrections for you guys with bifocals."

"Of course," Wayne nodded. "My problem wasn't a bad putter at all. It was a bad read because I couldn't see the subtle changes in the green. Zack, you've made my day. Thanks, partner."

Zack began to feel better, and appreciated any affirmation from a golfer of Wayne's caliber. Besides, with Zack's reading and Wayne's putting, they easily won the scramble!

***

During lunch, Hank elaborated, with help from Jorge, on the insights he had recently gained from IEE. He explained how Jorge had analyzed some of his data and showed that there was a common-cause problem that should be addressed head-on with an IEE project. After Hank and Jorge split the bill, they all walked together toward their cars.

Zack asked, "OK, I think I get it, but how does this affect my business?"

Ignoring Zack's question, Wayne interrupted, "You were making a point about IEE. Could you finish that?"

Jorge was glad to see that his friends were interested. He knew how exciting it could be to understand how powerful the IEE methodology really was.

"As I was saying," Hank stated proudly, "The primary success of Lean Six Sigma tends to be through projects that are selected by a steering committee. This all sounds good. However, often in deployments these projects do not have the true backing of the process owner and management. The thing is, these projects often are not only out of alignment with 'what' but also 'how' they are measured."

Wayne interrupted, "I'll co-sign that. What you are describing is exactly what I was experiencing!"

Hank continued, "This is not the case in an IEE deployment since it is a business management system that focuses on building upon your value chain with a no-nonsense measurement system that addresses not only 'what,', but also 'how' you report measurements. In addition, there is a structured approach with detailed roadmaps that guide you through both an enterprise business system and improvement project execution. Improvement projects will be supported by their process owner and management since they understand that the completion of these projects is necessary for them to achieve their goals. Projects are orchestrated across functions.

"Our IEE training for management and employees is going to change how they do their jobs. For the first time, I feel like we have control over our business. Well, control is probably too strong a word, but we understand where our problems are and have a roadmap to eliminate them. This applies to all areas of the business from marketing to manufacturing to customer service.

> For the first time, I feel like we have control over our business. Well, control is probably too strong a word, but we understand where our problems are and have a roadmap to eliminate them. This applies to all areas of the business from marketing to manufacturing to customer service.

"So, Zack, when you said you inherited a loser, that just makes your opportunities that much greater. You'll be able to make big improvements quickly, and you'll be the hero."

Hank continued, "There are people who do great things with their organizations. The problem is that the gains can't be maintained when the person leaves. Results are dependent on the person. That is why I used to reorganize so often. I was looking for those special people. With IEE, getting results becomes ingrained in the system and not in the person. The key is to find executives and managers who can execute the IEE business strategy. They don't have to be super heroes; after all, there are only so many of those."

As they reached his SUV, Jorge said, "Well, here we are again. We can now put another good day on the golf course in the record book. Tell you what. Now that you are all up to speed on what I have been doing up till last month, I'll treat you to breakfast tomorrow and elaborate on my more recent events."

"Wow, we can hardly wait," Wayne, Zack, and Hank echoed.

9

Improvement

... Practice the Full Swing

Choose a 7-iron or a 6-iron, whichever one you feel the most confidence in, and use it for 80 percent of all your full-swing practice....

The best way to learn to trust your swing is by practicing your swing with a club you trust.

Harvey Penick's Little Red Book (Penick with Shrake 1992)

Breakfast the Next Day

They all knew what they wanted to order for breakfast the next morning, so Jorge jumped right in, "As Hank and I described earlier, IEE uses an E-DMAIC process to analyze the business as a system. When the value chain 30,000-foot-level improvement needs pull for project creation, it only makes sense that the process owner and management will be interested in project completion.

Earlier, we talked about the define and measure phases in the P-DMAIC roadmap. Let's now discuss the analyze phase. In this phase, we work from Wisdom of the Organization listings that give us initial thoughts on where improvement opportunities might reside. We conduct passive analyses to determine the inputs that may impact our key process output variables or KPOVs. Inputs that affect our outputs are called key process input variables or KPIVs. In engineering terms, we could describe this relationship through the equation $Y=f(x)$. Y would be a KPOV, while x is a KPIV. Teams use Wisdom of the Organization to prioritize all the potential inputs and decide which to study further. The tools used here include cause-and-effect diagrams, cause-and-effect matrices, and FMEAs.

To test the relationship of our perceived KPIVs, our black belts use graphical analysis and statistical tools, such as: multi-vari charts, analysis of variance, and regression analysis. At first, when I reviewed black belt projects, I referred frequently to the P-DMAIC project execution roadmap from my training manual in order to know what tool was most appropriate. It's a great way to learn about the tools. After only a few times, tool usage became second nature.

I'm currently reviewing the project we discussed on days sales outstanding or DSO. The Wisdom of the Organization on this project gave us many potential KPIVs. However, there were some low-hanging-fruit issues that could be easily rectified; for example, getting all the billing departments to follow a single procedure.

"When we did this, our 30,000-foot-level control chart shifted to a new improved region of stability. We also did some statistical analyses that quantified, with a confidence interval, our potential for long-term improvement."

"What is a confidence interval?" Zack interrupted.

"Confidence intervals are like those reported during elections, when they give a margin of error. Confidence intervals are important because they quantify the uncertainties related to making statements from samples," Jorge explained.

Zack said, "You know, I think that happened to me the other day. We made a process change that we thought would make an improvement. We felt good when we ran a couple trials, and it looked like there was an improvement. However, I'm not convinced that the process really changed. It seems like the changes we saw were from common variation."

Zack elaborated, "It is unfortunate that we do not have a 30,000-foot-level metric chart reporting format as a baseline so we could see what happened over the long haul. The sad point is, we made some very expensive changes to our process and we don't have a clue whether the changes were beneficial or detrimental at the enterprise level. By the time we are finally able to tell for sure, we may have spent a lot of money and wasted a lot of time."

"Zack, you're right on," Hank said. "I think this happens a lot. Without IEE, you can be answering the wrong question. Previously we all had our own biases on what was causing defects in the printed circuit manufacturing process. When we let our prejudices about processes guide us without conducting a statistical analysis, it often led to major cost implications."

> Without IEE, you can be answering the wrong question. Previously we all had our own biases on what was causing defects in the printed circuit manufacturing process. When we let our prejudices about processes guide us without conducting a statistical analysis, it often led to major cost implications.

Jorge continued, "We followed the P-DMAIC roadmap for the DSO metric for our invoicing process. Wisdom of the Organization led us to think that there might be a difference between companies invoiced. Also, we thought that the size of an invoice might make a difference. Our passive statistical analysis showed that the average DSO was significantly different between companies. However, the relationship between the size of the invoice and the DSO was not statistically significant."

"Jorge, you are beginning to sound like a statistician," Wayne joked.

Jorge responded, "I guess so—a little bit. I'm getting excited because I'm starting to see people make decisions based on information rather than on sketchy data and gut feel."

Hank then said, "Let me tell you about what happened to us on one of our projects. We used gage R&R (repeatability and reproducibility) to quantify the consistency of the measurement system in one of our projects. It's an area we often overlook, and we were extremely surprised by the results. Almost 40% of our total process variability was due to measurement variation. With the existing gage, we were often accepting bad parts and rejecting good parts. When we included the cost of rework, lost production, and replacing customer shipments, we calculated that this gage alone was costing us five million dollars a year. We never would have found this without a structured IEE methodology. We just assumed that as long as the gage was calibrated everything was okay. We never realized that calibration of the measurement system was only one part of the equation."

Wayne interrupted, "That is sort of like my eyes. They were not capable of measuring the break or the speed of a putt, so I was missing them in all directions. All of the money I wasted on new putters pales in comparison to the money I've lost to you guys because I couldn't see the line on the putting green. You will all be happy to know that I have an eye appointment next week, and I should be making a lot more putts soon."

Everyone groaned, but Hank thought about resurrecting his idea of sponsoring Wayne on the senior tour as an investment opportunity.

"Do you remember a couple months ago when I was having problems with transactional errors?" Zack asked.

Jorge laughingly responded, "Your ears must have been burning last week. Hank and I had a long discussion on how we thought your situation lends itself directly to IEE."

Zack responded, "If I could make some low-hanging-fruit improvements, I might get my job back or at least leave with some scrap of dignity—if I can make some quick improvements. What wisdom on the green did I miss?"

For the next few minutes, Hank and Jorge filled Zack in on the particulars of the conversation they had last month. They agreed to look at some of Zack's data and help him outline a strategy.

As they got up to leave the breakfast table, Jorge looked at Zack and offered, "Now that we have helped with Wayne's golf game, would you like a suggestion?"

Zack felt like he was on a roll here and responded, "Sure, shoot!"

"Well, Wayne's problem was not his putter, but his vision. Hank's problem was one of course management, that is making smarter club selections based not just on his best ever shot, but on the expected variation with different clubs."

"OK, but what about me?" Zack asked impatiently.

"Your problem is different. It's not any particular club, and it's certainly not physical. Your eyes are great, and your physique is good, too. Your problem is more basic," Jorge said. "Your problem is very fundamental. Your grip, your alignment, even your swing are all too much like your old baseball-playing days. As a result, you have processes with too much variation. Hooks, slices, topped shots, thin shots, a little of everything."

"I guess I should just give up the game then," Zack moaned.

"Not at all," said Jorge. "Actually, it's easy to fix. Just get a little coaching on the fundamentals of the stance, grip, and swing, and practice with your 7 iron until it feels natural. An hour with a pro and a few buckets of balls are all it will take for you to break 90 almost every time."

"But what about all the other clubs? Don't I need a new driver?" Zack questioned.

Jorge finished, "Don't worry about that now. Your problems are so fundamental that you can fix them without much effort. The 7 iron is the easiest to hit and will help you ingrain the fundamental changes quickly. Only then can you tell whether you really need to make any adjustments in your equipment. My guess is you won't need to make any."

"Wow," said Zack, "With all the help you're giving me in my business and my golf game, I'll have enough time to salvage my family life, too!"

10

Enlightenment

Chipping

The first and foremost fundamental to learn about chipping is this: keep your hands ahead of or even with the clubhead on the follow through. All the way through....

Always chip the ball if:
1. *The lie is poor.*
2. *The green is hard.*
3. *You have a downhill lie.*
4. *The wind has an influence on the shot.*
5. *You are under stress.*

Harvey Penick's Little Red Book (Penick with Shrake 1992)

October

With paper in hand, Jorge approached the boys on their way to the practice green. Excitedly, he called out, "Zack, we were right about your data. It appears to be a common-cause problem. A 30,000-foot-level control chart of your transactional errors indicates that your process is not changing. The up and down variation of the data is from the noise within your process. From the criteria that you sent me, I expect that you are firefighting about 10% of the time."

Zack said, "Hey, that seems right because we spend about two days a month chasing transactional entry errors that have error rates beyond our criterion. Let me see the chart."

Jorge gave Zack the printout and said, "The charts show that with your red-yellow-green scorecard system, you haven't really fixed anything. How much do you think that is costing your business?"

Zack shook his head in disbelief and then replied, "You sure know how to use data to hurt a guy's feelings. I don't have a clue how much this is costing the business, but I know it's not pretty!"

Hank suggested, "Zack, if you want to reduce the error rate, you could do some passive analyses, like we talked about last week, which might even lead to a DOE."

"DOE?" Zack asked, barely lifting his eyes from the control chart.

"DOE is short for Design of Experiments. I can explain it in more detail after we get some practice putts in. The rain last night probably slowed the greens down," Hank said, eager to play.

Zack had also found some time for a lesson with the pro, and everyone noticed his new swing even in the warm-ups on the first tee. His stance was square, his grip was neutral, and his smooth swing now looked more like Wayne's swing than they could ever have imagined. When Zack teed off, it was 250 yards on the fairway, with just a hint of draw. The others all commented that they might need to adjust handicaps for the group if this continued.

***

Waiting at the second tee, Wayne asked, "Did you finish the DSO project yet, Jorge?"

Jorge replied, "You may remember, our Wisdom of the Organization led us to examine the size of invoice and the customer invoiced. Passive analysis tools from our E-DMAIC roadmap led us to a statistically significant issue between customers. That is, the customer invoiced was identified as a key process input variable for DSO.

"We then brainstormed about what we might do differently to improve our DSO response. However, to validate these improvement ideas, we needed to execute some tests using Design of Experiments, as Hank mentioned earlier.

"We came up with a list of seven factors to evaluate during the DOE. Some of these factors were process noise variables such as from which hospital the invoice originated. We also included things we could change within our process, including billing formats. For the experiment, we set up each of the seven factors with two levels. For example, in the case of the factor-billing department there were two locations, 1 and 2. From our passive analyses earlier, we thought location number 1 did better and location number 2 did worse.

"If you consider all combinations of factors and levels, experiments can get to be very large. However, with fractional factorial DOE experimentation we used a subset of all combinations, and this reduced our number of tests from 128 to 16, while still obtaining very valuable information from our process."

"Oh, you get a free lunch for not having to do 128 trials," Zack remarked sarcastically.

Jorge responded, "Not exactly. When we conduct this type of experiment, we confound information about our interactions, but, this is not all bad since it saves us a lot of time. Before I get to that, I should describe what an interaction is. Remember the old copier machines in the 1970s?"

"That was way before my time," Zack bragged facetiously.

"Sure," Jorge replied dryly, "You're so much younger than the rest of us. Anyway, copier-feed failures were a major problem. Two KPIVs were ambient temperature and humidity. If you compared feed failure rates at 68 and 98 degrees at low humidity, no change was noticeable. However, at high humidity if you compare feed failure rates at either 68 degrees or 98 degrees, a significant change is indicated. Feed failures were higher when both the humidity and the temperature were high. This means that there was interaction between the two factors, temperature and humidity. The real problem source was that the moisture in the air was the highest at this condition, which resulted in water absorption of the paper and feed problems. You cannot understand the effect of these factors without looking at both of them together."

Jorge continued, "If an interaction exists within our process, we may never find the solution by changing one factor at a time. A well-structured DOE manages the confounding of two-factor interactions. Anyway, there is too much detail to get involved with DOE on the golf course. You need much of a week's black belt training to understand fully the benefits of DOE and how to plan them efficiently. But, it is a very powerful strategy applicable to many situations."

***

As the match progressed, Jorge realized that everyone was playing better today. He was keeping his shots in play and using his short game to great effect around the greens. At the turn, he was out in 38, and Hank thought his way to an intelligent 39 with no penalty strokes. Wayne made several putts wearing his new glasses for a one-under 35, and Jorge wondered what would happen after the laser surgery that was scheduled in a few days. Even Zack demonstrated remarkable variation reduction with his new swing and shot 44 on the front. The match stood even, but Jorge realized they were all 'winning.'

***

Waiting at the turn, Wayne asked, "So are DOE techniques applicable to all projects?"

"Not always," Hank responded. "All Six Sigma and Lean tools have applications, and each of them should be used when most appropriate. However, DOE techniques are very beneficial, both to manufacturing and transactional situations."

Hank continued, "It's like in golf, where there are usually several ways to hit a shot. Some are easier to hit than others. Some have less variability in their results, like Jorge talks about.

"Picking the right tool is always important. For our DSO project, we conducted a DOE where we considered seven factors. During our passive analysis, we found that there were two groups of customers: those who making timely payments and those who were chronically late. We treated this as one of our seven factors. Another factor we looked at was whether or not we gave the customer a reminder call a week after invoicing."

As they approached the tenth green, Jorge sliced his approach shot more to the right than normal. When they found the ball, it was about four feet directly behind a medium-sized tree with a forked trunk and low-hanging branches. Wayne and Zack feigned disappointment at Jorge's lot.

"Looks like that tree has you stymied," said Zack with a heavy dose of mock sympathy.

"Yeah, I guess it's up to you on this hole, partner," Jorge said to Hank.

"Maybe not," said Hank as he looked at the shot more carefully.

Jorge was directly behind the tree, and the base of the eight-inch trunk blocked his path to the hole while overhanging branches restricted the shot selection to a height of less than five feet. However, Hank noticed that the natural 'V' in the trunk left an opening to the flag that was almost three feet wide at the top and narrowed down to nothing at ground level.

Hank said, "Look at this! You're back far enough that you can chip right through the fork of this tree with your 5 iron. That should keep it down below the branches, but get it up just enough to go through the 'V' in the trunk. Bump it into the face of the green, and it should run right up to the hole. You can still get it up and down!"

Zack and Wayne taunted Jorge as he lined up the shot, but their jeers turned to cheers of amazement as he executed an almost perfect bump and run shot, exactly as instructed.

"Thanks for the 'GET OUT OF JAIL FREE' card, partner. How do you come up with such creative ideas?" Jorge asked with a satisfied grin.

Hank answered, "Good judgment. You know, it comes from experience, and experience comes from bad judgment. My length gets me into a lot of trouble on the course. I've been in so many tough situations that I've learned to be creative. I just used my extensive Wisdom of the Organization to pick the right tool for the job.

"The best thing about being a teacher is that I learn so much!" Hank said as he punctuated his comment by tapping in his miracle par putt.

As they all moved to the next tee, Jorge continued his discussion, "Through DOE, we discovered that our late customers were paying sooner, on average, when they received reminder calls a week after they were initially invoiced. The companies that normally pay on time showed no change when they received reminders. This is an example of the kind of interaction we talked about earlier. Because of this objective data, we were able to motivate change in the process. For our new process, we will have a reminder call, one week after invoicing, only for those companies that are historically delinquent. As you can imagine, this will save us a lot of time and money. In addition, our good-paying clients won't get frustrated with our phone calls."

Hank added, "In our circuit board defect-reduction project, the passive analysis tools led us to a significant issue of cleanliness within our printed circuit board manufacturing process. Cleanliness was identified as a KPIV for the defect rate KPOV. We then brainstormed for what we might do differently to improve cleanliness. In order to validate these improvement ideas, we need to perform some tests. That's where we'll be using DOE, the way Jorge has been describing."

As the round ended, the match ended up even, but the entire group felt like winners. Everyone had played well, with Wayne shooting par 72, Hank a 79, Jorge 80, and even Zack broke through with an 89. As they drove to their cars to deposit their clubs, Jorge thought that this was not just a random combination of unlikely occurrences. This was more likely an example of real systemic improvement in everyone's game.

***

As they reached his SUV, Jorge suggested, "I hate to bring this up, but this approach could also help Zack improve the effectiveness of a potential project that he has not discussed yet."

"What project is that?" Zack asked.

"Doesn't your financial company send out junk mail to solicit business?" Jorge replied.

Zack tersely responded, "We prefer to view this activity as a mass mailing."

"Given what we've discussed about DOE, don't you think you could use these techniques to improve the response rate from your mass mailings?" Jorge quizzed.

"Maybe it would help and could even improve my standing with our CEO. How would it work exactly?" Zack replied.

Jorge responded, "Well, you would basically follow the process that we did for our projects. When you get to the point of asking yourself what should be done differently, there will probably be differences of opinion. Let's consider that one idea was sending a very large post card instead of an envelope for your mass mailings. This would be cheaper than sending a letter and might stand out better against all the other junk mail."

"Mass mail," Zack corrected.

"Anyway," Jorge started laughing, "Before you change to this new marketing strategy, you'd want to test its effectiveness."

"Hey, Jorge," Wayne interrupted, "Why don't you install a projector in your SUV so you can do a presentation when we have class out here in the parking lot?"

Jorge ignored the laughter and continued, "With a traditional approach, we would send out trial post cards and compare the number of responses we get to what we had previously. This approach can cause problems. There is a time delay between the change and response. Also, something else could have happened in the economy to affect our responses. That would be considered a confounding effect. To compare the envelope mailing with the post card approach, we would have to send out some envelopes and some post cards during the same time frame."

"That would be easy to do and give us valuable information on our process," Zack agreed.

Jorge responded, "Great. We could do this and then compare the responses statistically. However, I believe that there might be other factors that should be considered at the same time, such as time of the month that the mailing goes out, your mailing list source, and maybe if the recipient is male or female?"

Zack then said, "All of these factors could make a difference."

Jorge responded, "If that's the case, they all should be considered within the DOE."

Zack asked, "But won't that mix things up?"

"Not if the experiment is conducted correctly. When you get back to the office, give me a call. I'll show you a reference that illustrates this point vividly," Jorge responded.

Wayne jumped in, stating, "You know I think that DOE could help within our product development process."

Jorge responded, "That's right. Within an IEE DMADV process, DOEs can be very beneficial. You could use a DOE to evaluate structurally various combinations of input conditions that might affect a response. You could assess these factors in a structured way, combining manufacturing conditions with customer applications. This would help you select the best combination of factor settings to give the best results for your customers. You can also use DOE techniques to develop a test strategy for new products. When I get back to the office, I'll also give you a reference example from our Lean Six Sigma textbook that illustrates how DOE can be useful in development organizations. The bottom line is: Whenever you are considering testing something, consider DOE."

> That's right. Within an IEE DMADV process, DOEs can be very beneficial. You could use a DOE to evaluate structurally various combinations of input conditions that might affect a response.

Zack said, "Sounds like DOE can be very useful."

Then Jorge said, "Not to change the subject, but I was thinking about what Hank said last month about Gage R&R. We're not currently taking this on as a project: however, many of the tests within hospitals are executed and interpreted as though there are no testing errors. This is especially alarming when we state that tests for AIDS are either positive or negative. In either case, if we are wrong, the consequences to the patients and their families can be devastating."

Hank responded. "I think that all industries should be more sensitive to Gage R&R and measurement error. When measurement variation is unsatisfactory, we can make wrong decisions. For example, our court system is a measurement system for evaluating guilt. And, it's subject to errors. Now with DNA testing, the measurement system has improved."

Wayne said, "You've sold me. I'm going to set up a meeting with our CEO to discuss how we'll roll out IEE."

With that, four happy and relaxed golfers headed home with hopes for continued improvement.

11

Making Progress

November

It was a beautiful November day, nice enough that Zack had the top down on his convertible as he pulled into the course parking lot. Today he was looking good and feeling good.

The first thing out of Zack's mouth when he saw Hank at the practice green was, "I expected to see you at the driving range. Are you taking Jorge's advice and practicing your weaknesses instead of your strengths?" When Hank just smiled and ignored him, he tried, "From the IEE book you recommended on the phone, I can really see how the structure of DOE does not confound individual factors."

Hank just smiled again, thinking about Zack, the stylish analytic.

Wayne, who was also putting, said, "Hank, I really see now, from the example you pointed out over the phone, how DOE techniques can be beneficial in the development process. Those real examples were very insightful. I can see how examples from the books used during IEE training can help communicate specific application techniques to suppliers and customers who have not yet taken the training."

Zack added, "I am thinking about how so many companies have product recall problems. It's happening in the automobile and computer industries quite regularly. Why aren't they using IEE?"

"Interesting you said that, Zack," said Jorge as he arrived on the scene. "I've wondered the same thing. Many of these companies would say that they are implementing Lean Six Sigma if you ask them. There must be hundreds, if not thousands, of Lean Six Sigma providers now popping up all over. I have to wonder how many of these providers are just jumping on the bandwagon. I wonder how many of these deployments truly address business needs."

Jorge said, "Let me tell you what happened last month with the two projects that I've been describing. With both projects, we have identified some key process inputs that are driving our key process output. We changed our processes so that the drivers would give the most consistent response possible. In some cases, we were able to mistake-proof the process. In others, we created 50-foot-level control charts. A frequent sampling plan with these charts allowed us to identify when a shift occurred so we could fix the problem before there was too much water under the bridge, so to speak.

"In both projects, the 30,000-foot-level metrics went out-of-control to the better. The process capability now looks good. We are going to track this overall process output continuously. At some later date, there might be another KPIV interjected so that our overall output is degraded. With this chart, we want to be able to quickly identify when this happens so that we can take appropriate action," Jorge said.

"You know, I have not really mentioned this before," Hank said, "But I found that the soft-skill training we received to be very useful. It involved people skills such as team building and change management. We also covered some creativity and project management skills."

Zack then asked, "Do you have any lessons you'd like to share from your first wave of training, Jorge?"

Jorge said, "Yes, I do. For one thing, we think that we could do a better job determining who would be the best black belt candidates. Also, we need to work at better scoping the size of our projects, and some of our metrics on some projects were not as good as they could have been. Also, we need to work on achieving a standard report-out format. And, we want to have our suppliers more involved with our next wave of black belt training."

Zack responded, "Where are you going to go from here, Jorge?"

Jorge replied, "Well, as I mentioned in an earlier outing, we've created a function called Enterprise Process Management or EPM. This function is making great progress refining our internal process for executing E-DMAIC. When the black belts complete their current projects, they will be moving on to others. Currently, it looks like the 20 black belts who were, or will be, in the public workshop at our provider's facility will create a total annual benefit of about ten million dollars."

Zack said, "Guess that got your CEO's attention."

Jorge said, "It sure did. However, that is somewhat the small gain from the overall IEE deployment. We now have a value chain system and monthly metric reporting that is leading to the right activities at the right time. Our firefighting has definitely decreased. Our CEO is not only planning to carry the financial savings numbers forward to the board of directors, but also to present our overall IEE system and how it has improved how we do business. She plans to put something in our annual report about the system and the benefits we have achieved for our customers and our shareholders."

Zack then said, "You know how I wanted to get some face time with our CEO? Well, I could not get on his calendar. It seems like he was too busy."

Wayne said, "I was able to get in touch with our CEO at Wonder-Chem, but I don't believe that he shared my enthusiasm. He told me to get with the education department to discuss it."

Jorge said, "I want to re-emphasize that I am sure glad we have our CEO on board. She is very receptive and listens to our suggestions. She is getting to the point where she is asking us the right questions. As for your point, Wayne, I am really concerned about rollouts through the education department. This does not mean that this strategy will not work, but the image of a deployment when it originates from the education department is that just a bunch of tools will be taught. From this arena, it will be difficult to get visibility that the deployment is most successful when it is a part of the strategy of a business and rolled out through those areas which are actually doing the operational tasks within a company."

Jorge continued, "And Zack, how about refocusing the intent of your meeting with your CEO? Build a case for IEE by going back and collecting some of your major business metrics. I can help you present the data in a 30,000-foot-level format. We can then make a rough pass at the cost of doing nothing differently, or CODND metrics. I'll bet that your CEO will have a 180 degree change in perspective after seeing our findings."

Hank responded, "I agree completely with Jorge. I have learned a lesson about selling IEE, too. Talk the language your CEO likes to hear; money and what relieves their pain."

***

The round of golf that followed was another good one, or, as Jorge would have described it, a second set of scores as a process shift on the good side using a 30,000-foot-level tracking control chart strategy.

For the first time in a long time, there was almost no discussion of business during the round or the dinner that followed.

It was good to relax.

12

The 19th Hole

"Take Dead Aim!"

... This is a wonderful thought to keep in mind all the way around the course, not just on the first tee. Take dead aim at a spot on the fairway or the green, refuse to allow any negative thought to enter your head, and swing away.

Harvey Penick's Little Red Book (Penick with Shrake 1992)

December

Zack was running to catch up with the others at the first tee. He called ahead excitedly, "When I took the metrics into our CEO and showed him how the CODND was running at least 20% of our gross income, he suddenly got interested. Now I have a new job. I will be leading the corporation's new IEE Strategy. Our rollout starts next month. This is going to be fun!"

Jorge responded. "I'm looking forward to hearing your story in the upcoming months. I must warn you though, my consulting fees will be going up considerably if you get promoted."

"That's OK," Zack smiled. "Now I have some control over my game's KPIVs. You know, my grip, stance, and swing basics—we'll win enough golf bets to pay for them."

Zack's first tee shot backed up his boast; a nice draw about 240 yards in the left center of the fairway.

Stepping up to the tee, Wayne said, "I had a similar experience when I set up another meeting with our CEO and started speaking his language. When I put the advantages in terms of money and pain relief, he bought in immediately. We are setting up the infrastructure to start our IEE rollout next month as well."

> When I put the advantages in terms of money and pain relief, he bought in immediately.

Hank smiled, "Ah yes, the universal language of business executives has always been considered to be money. But pain relief also needs to be ranked up there, also."

Wayne continued, "I agree with Zack. After my eye surgery, I'm seeing so much better ... reading the greens and judging distances. We'll be winning more bets and collecting more of that 'money portion of the universal language' from you two."

Wayne followed up his comments with boring precision. His drive was another ho-hum performance off the tee, 265 yards straight down the middle in the perfect location.

Jorge commented, "Looks like we better step it up, partner."

Hank teed his ball. With plenty of room to work within the fairway, he hit a monster drive that airmailed Wayne and Zack, leaving him in perfect birdie position.

Hank said, "You may want to check your credit limits to see if they can handle a dinner tab after all."

Jorge then hit his soft fade down the middle a few yards behind Zack's ball. He was the short hitter off the tee, but from this position in the fairway, he knew that he was actually ahead of the game. He hit first from the fairway, putting his 5 wood on the green, and the pressure back firmly on the others in the group.

Jorge commented, "You know, I just realized that we are all enjoying our game much more. We all seem to be under a lot less stress."

***

In fact, Hank had resolved his Mexican production problems and had moved on to big, new cost savings from his IEE program, making Hi-tech very competitive on price while still trading on their high-quality reputation. Hank had just been named senior vice president with new corporate-wide business improvement responsibilities. It meant fewer day-to-day headaches and more time for golf and maybe even a family life again.

Wayne had leveraged IEE at Wonder-Chem, building on the previous Lean Six Sigma training, to create a strong competitive advantage in over-the-counter health care products. Now he was excited about executing the DMADV portion of the IEE roadmap and its potential to improve R&D and reduce product development times. It had turned out that not only was money a universal language component for CEOs, but time was also money.

Zack was also making personal progress as corporate IEE champion for Z-Credit. He was finding a fertile market for business improvement in the financial sector and was beginning to build a reputation as a fast tracker again. He was even getting home most evenings before his wife and kids went to bed!

As for Jorge, he was proud that he had been able to improve Harris Hospital's performance in such a short period of time. It seemed like activities were now more orchestrated. He had kept his promise to provide his patients with the best care possible at the lowest possible cost. Now he spent most of his time coaching teams that apply the IEE strategy, instead of fighting managerial fires. "Isn't it great to love your job!" he thought.

***

At the end of the round, when the group met at Jorge's SUV in the parking lot, everyone looked at Jorge as Hank asked, "So when is our next golf date?"

Wayne and Zack chimed in, "Yes, and what's our next lesson, Professor Jorge?"

Appendix: Articles

A.1 Common [Six Sigma] Problems (and what to do about them)

The following is reproduced from the *Six Sigma Forum Magazine* (Breyfogle 2005). In the article, a Six Sigma deployment was referenced; however, the same concepts are applicable to a Lean Six Sigma deployment. An IEE deployment addresses these issues head-on.

Six Sigma deployments don't always run smoothly, so I compiled a list of 21 frequently encountered situations. You've likely come across at least one but may not have known how best to handle it—until now.

1. My organization started its Six Sigma deployment five years ago, and now we're having difficulty finding projects, especially projects of value. It appears as if projects in this Six Sigma deployment are being sought out by the Six Sigma steering committee, even though the process owners have no true urgency for project initiation and completion. It would be better to have a deployment system where process owners solicit help that leads to the execution of Six Sigma projects, which help their business-aligned performance metrics.

2. Our program stalled after our Six Sigma deployment executive left. A dictatorship can be great if the dictator truly understands what is needed and addresses those needs without bureaucracy. Even if this utopia were to exist, major chaos would probably result after the dictator's departure.

Organizations need a Six Sigma deployment that is not solely dependent on one executive's drive. They need to create a system where the process owner asks for the creation of Six Sigma projects to improve their performance metrics, which are aligned with business needs. This should happen no matter which executive is in place.

3. A black belt (BB) or master black belt (MBB) certification would look good on my résumé. What's the easiest way to get one? Organizations should focus on having the best people learn how to wisely apply Six Sigma and Lean techniques to improve performance measures and better meet customer needs. A deployment that focuses on belt titles for the masses rather than results does not accomplish this.

4. In our Six Sigma deployment, managers are measured by the number of employees trained and their validated financial savings. With this strategy, people in all functions seek out the least painful training and the easiest projects that will provide them Six Sigma project credit. Minimal, if any, attention is given to targeting improvement efforts that impact the primary business success constraints.

5. Our organization will be doing Lean, then Six Sigma. Lean and Six Sigma tool usage should depend on the business and its associated metric improvement needs. A deployment rollout should address both tool sets simultaneously with a high-level operational metric system that pulls for the right tool at the right time.

6. Our organization will have Six Sigma trainees complete an easy classroom project in which they can use the tools. Later they can apply the methods to projects that are more important to the business. This type of statement says training is the primary focus of the Six Sigma deployment. Instead, the organization should focus on executing projects that improve the overall enterprise metrics.

7. Jack Welch did it wrong at General Electric (GE). He should have leaned out all business units instead of selling the business units he did not want to deal with. Lean is a very powerful tool; however, not all businesses are profitable or aligned with the organization's mission. In a Six Sigma deployment, data should help a business decide where it can best focus its efforts and resources, even if that means it has to sell certain business units. Therefore, I believe Jack Welch did the right thing by selling the businesses that were not aligned with their overall business needs.

8. Our organization is going to do 5S (sort, straighten, shine, standardize, and sustain) first and then move on to Six Sigma. An organization could have a clean and efficient process to make something no one buys. Instead, it needs to create a system in which the best Lean or Six Sigma tools are used to improve business metrics and synthesize voice of the customer inputs to targeted actions. Tools such as 5S need to be applied within a Six Sigma deployment, when they are most applicable.

9. Our company is going to conduct a pilot project to see if Six Sigma works before considering a deployment. This sounds like a great starting point; however, a pilot project can fail for a number of reasons, including non-dedicated resource people who don't have the time to work on a project that is not important to the process owner.

The success or failure of a specific project is not a good test of whether Six Sigma works. Wisely applied Six Sigma with Lean works if activities are aligned to business operational metrics needs. The real question is, "What can be done to ensure an organization maximizes its benefits from the concepts of Six Sigma?"

10. Our team was told a successful Six Sigma deployment must have the CEO's buy-in. Not all CEOs have the personality and drive Jack Welch did when he kicked off Six Sigma at GE. Also, some CEOs may have had a poor introduction to Six Sigma and need to be shown how the wise application of Six Sigma and Lean tools can directly address their business needs. Executive buy-in is no excuse for not advocating a wise deployment of Six Sigma with Lean and effective performance measures. Advocacy selling may be the first step toward jump starting a deployment.

11. Our Six Sigma project benefits are measured in hard savings, and we're having a difficult time determining the cost benefits for design for Six Sigma projects and those that address voice of the customer needs. Six Sigma deployments that focus only on hard savings can lead to the wrong activities. This organization needs metrics and a deployment system that pulls for the creation of the right activity at the right time.

12. Our organization is trying to follow a define, measure, analyze, improve, control (DMAIC) roadmap for just-do-it situations. An organization's culture and metrics should lead to the right tool selection at the right time to improve overall enterprise metrics needs. Not all improvements need be in the form of a formalized DMAIC project. A wisely created Six Sigma deployment system addresses this systematic business improvement need.

13.   Everyone knows which easy to implement change needs to be made, but our Six Sigma coach says we still need to apply regression analysis and design of experiments to the project. In a wisely created Six Sigma deployment system, it is okay to immediately implement agree-to, low-hanging fruit changes that are thought beneficial to the overall system. High-level control charts can assess whether implemented changes have altered key process output variable levels, while statistical tests can address significance levels. When a significant change is demonstrated, overall comparisons can then be made to the project's overall expectations.

It is important to avoid analysis paralysis. There is nothing wrong with implementing just-do-it projects and monitoring the success of the implementation.

14.   Our organization is going to hire new BBs and MBBs rather than train people who are already part of the organization. This is a compelling strategy; however, finding someone who has the right skill set and can fit into a company's culture is easier said than done. It is more preferable to develop those within an organization who have the right BB or MBB personality profile, have already established internal relationships for getting things done and possess the wisdom of organizational understanding.

15.   We are in the process of selecting a Six Sigma provider. Selecting the best Six Sigma provider for an organization can be confusing. Sales pitches that sound good may not always lead to the best selection. It is important to understand the provider's basic strategy and project execution roadmap before deciding who to go with. Also, organizations need to ensure the Six Sigma organization practices what it preaches.

16.   I want to earn my green belt, BB, or MBB certification by taking an e-learning class. Building a skill set to answer predefined questions is not difficult. The hard part is defining the right problems to solve. These techniques are learned through classroom and coaching sessions where much of the dialogue centers on specific, real-life issues.

17. I am going to attend a local Six Sigma class to save money. It is more important to pick the Six Sigma deployment strategy and training that best fulfills an organization's needs.

18. Our team is going to start deployment in manufacturing and then move to transactional processes. This strategy can lead to the suboptimization of processes. The first thing an organization should do is assess the big picture and identify any constraints. The initial projects should focus on these constraints, no matter where they come from. For example, if an organization's main constraint is sales, then the first projects should focus on that.

19. Our organization is going to save money by developing its own Six Sigma course material, where all examples will be tailored to our company. We will also save money by using newly trained BBs and MBBs to conduct these sessions. Organizations can easily be penny wise and pound foolish when it comes to Six Sigma training material development. It takes years of continual improvements to develop effective Six Sigma material and an associated roadmap.

Internal BB and MBB resources should initially focus on the creation of an infrastructure that pulls for the creation and completion of projects. Having internal BBs and MBBs conduct initial training detracts from this focus. In course material, it is important for students to learn how to bridge examples to their situations. With this knowledge, they will later be able to understand how to apply articles written about other industries to their situations.

20. Our team is having difficulty determining which tool to use when. Tool selection is important but it can be confusing to novices. It is important to have and use Six Sigma project execution roadmaps combined with effective coaching. This will help a team choose the right tool for the situation at hand.

21. In our Six Sigma training, our team was instructed to describe the process capability for all projects using metrics such as sigma quality level, Cp, Cpk, Pp, and Ppk. These metrics are not used in our day-to-day process work. The terminology used in the execution of projects should use day-to-day metric descriptions that everyone, from the line operators to the CEO, understands. Any confusing and misleading Six Sigma metrics should be avoided (Breyfogle 2003).

Peter Senge (Senge 1990) writes that learning disabilities are tragic in children but fatal in organizations. Because of them, few corporations live even half as long as a person—most die before they reach the age of 40. "Learning organizations" defy these odds and overcome learning disabilities to understand threats and recognize new opportunities. If we choose to break a complex system into many elements, the optimization of each element does not typically lead to total system optimization; e.g., optimizing purchasing costs by choosing cheaper parts can impact manufacturing costs through an increase in defect rates. Organizations need to create a Six Sigma system that avoids optimizing subsystems at the expense of the overall system. With systems thinking we do not lose sight of the big picture. Wise Six Sigma deployments offer a roadmap for changing data into knowledge that leads to new opportunities. Through a wise Six Sigma deployment, organizations can become a learning organization!

A.2 Starting a Six Sigma Initiative

The following was reproduced from ISixSigma "Ask the Expert" (Breyfogle 2004). In the article a Six Sigma deployment was referenced; however, the same concepts are applicable to a Lean Six Sigma deployment. An IEE deployment addresses these issues head-on.

Q: What can an organization establishing an Office of Six Sigma/Quality learn from the companies which have been most successful at setting up such offices? How did those companies go about it and with how many people typically?

Successful implementations of Six Sigma simply view purpose as $E = MC^2$; i.e., organization's **E**xistence/**E**xcellence equates to **M**ore **C**ustomers and **C**ash. The office title and all efforts need to be directed toward this goal.

Full deployment is often suggested as the best way to initiate Six Sigma; however, it is typically better to grow into an overall system. In the real world, most companies don't have the bandwidth to create an infrastructure that can support a very large instantaneous Six Sigma deployment.

A small but committed force of the right people given the proper authority can do wonders to get things started. Companies which are successful implement a system that builds upon the lessons learned and successes of others. Approaching initial implementation of Six Sigma through a pilot program has advantages; however, it is essential at the onset that the right people are involved, doing the right things.

Companies that have successfully implemented Six Sigma share some basic characteristics—committed leadership, use of top talent and a supporting infrastructure. This supporting infrastructure involved creating a formal project selection process, a formal project review process, dedicated resources and financial system integration.

However, the Six Sigma implementation team can encounter significant resource restrictions. Frequently, a major limitation is that only part-time resources are to be used. This can lead to the training of green belts or black belts, who will have little, if any, infrastructure support. Teaching Six Sigma and Lean tools without the suggested infrastructure will not provide a satisfactory evaluation of Six Sigma. Successful Six Sigma deployments also are a function of infrastructure. Hence, a pilot assessment not only needs one or more Six Sigma projects, but also must include dedicated resources and a formal project review process. To assure this, top-level management should agree at the outset that the pilot program will include a Six Sigma infrastructure modeled after other successful deployments, and will include well-defined measures to judge the pilot project's success.

As part of this pilot program, a Six Sigma steering committee needs to be created to manage the overall Six Sigma process. A Six Sigma director, who is well respected change agent within the company, should be chosen. He/she needs to believe in the concept of Six Sigma and have the drive to make Six Sigma successful. The Six Sigma director needs to be a dedicated resource. Exceptions to this rule are justified only for small organizations.

The steering committee should carefully select two to ten employees who will be trained in a public black belt workshop, where each trainee is a dedicated resource for the completion of assigned projects. Regularly scheduled on-site and/or remote coaching sessions also are conducted between four separate weeks of training. A project coaching session also should include the project's champion, team members, and process owner.

The sessions could be conducted remotely but the frequency of coaching should emulate a full-scale deployment; e.g., weekly report-outs. Scheduled monthly executive presentation times should be established where the steering committee, sometimes with the aid of teams, presents the Six Sigma pilot status with quantifiable results.

Upon completion of a successful Six Sigma pilot, the scale of the deployment is simply expanded to other areas of the business, incorporating any lessons learned from the pilot session.

Q: What magnitude of resources/dollars should be committed for the first three years of a Six Sigma initiative? Is there a rule of thumb?

If Six Sigma costs anything, something is wrong. Six Sigma is an investment upon which organization and personal existence/excellence depends. When Six Sigma is implemented correctly, it should yield a return of at least 20 times the investment in three years.

When setting up an infrastructure, companies can easily become penny wise and pound foolish. For example, companies might insist on saving money by using black belts who are part time. With this approach, projects can fall off the black belt's plate, resulting in project completion difficulties. Companies can achieve a much larger return on investment with dedicated resources. It is important to get the right people involved doing the right things.

In addition, organizations need to view Six Sigma as an implementation methodology that does more than just pick and complete projects. The implementation of Six Sigma must impact how people think and perform their day-to-day work. Wisely applied, Six Sigma metrics and improvement strategies can get organizations out of the firefighting mode and into the fire-prevention mode. For this to happen, organizations need to measure the right thing and then report it in a fashion that leads to the right activity.

Q: Does a Six Sigma organization need to be run by a master black belt or a black belt to be effective?

Making it a requirement that the leader of a Six Sigma organization be or become a master black belt or black belt can lead to the selection of the wrong person.

The leader of a Six Sigma organization needs to be familiar with the tools and methodologies of Six Sigma and Lean. He/she needs:

- To be able to look at the big picture and orchestrate activities that get the right people involved doing the right things.
- To be able to ask the right questions.
- To be able to motivate people so that projects are completed in a timely fashion.

- To understand the overall Six Sigma project execution, step-by-step roadmap and check sheets for project completion. (This understanding is necessary so that he/she can lead practitioners into doing and completing the right tasks in a timely manner.)
- To practice and demonstrate Six Sigma methodologies in his/her day-to-day activities.
- To be able to understand and convey the methodologies and benefits of Six Sigma to others.

A high mark in all the above skill-set categories is hard to find in any one individual. Real-time coaching of a Six Sigma leader who has all the right interpersonal relationship skills can be an effective compromise. With this approach, a Six Sigma coach works with the leader on the improvement of his skills so that he/she asks the right question; e.g., directing a practitioner to the correct Six Sigma or Lean application tool. This approach can be more effective than hiring or reassigning a black belt or master black belt to run the operation.

Q: Should a new Six Sigma initiative be promoted by upper management? If so, how would you recommend it be communicated?

Advocacy selling of Six Sigma can originate at any organizational level; however, the effectiveness of such promotion increases when originated at the executive level.

It has been said that the only reason people change is either to seek pleasure or avoid pain, where stimulus from avoiding pain is larger than seeking pleasure. GE employed both of these methods in their rollout of Six Sigma. People had to change or they would be terminated—the painful stick. In addition, a system was set up so that people who accomplished tangible results with Six Sigma were rewarded—the carrot. Similarly, in the $E=MC^2$ model, the letter E represented Existence (i.e., the stick) and/or Excellence (i.e., the carrot).

The creation of a burning platform—a visible crisis—is an effective approach to convey the importance of instituting systematic improvements to the enterprise. The necessity of change should be presented in such a way that it is not only easy to understand, but also readily internalized.

The presentation should show that when there is an alignment of Six Sigma work with business needs and/or operational metrics both existence and bottom-line excellence can be achieved.

A.3 Exercises

1. After reading the article, "Common Six Sigma Problems (and what to do about them)," comment on five points that you think could have the biggest impact in a Six Sigma deployment.
2. Comment on the following after reading the article, "Starting a Six Sigma initiative."
   a. Describe what companies should focus on when implementing IEE.
   b. Describe an alternative to a full Lean Six Sigma deployment and why this strategy should be considered.
   c. Describe the basic characteristics of companies that have a successful implementation.
   d. State how much IEE implementation should cost.
   e. Give an example of how companies can become penny wise and pound foolish.
   f. Describe the characteristics of a leader of IEE in an organization.
   g. Describe an effective approach to convey the importance of implementing IEE.

Glossary

Address: The final position, stance, and actions just before the golf swing begins.

Alignment: The position of the golfer's body and clubface in relation to the target line.

Analysis of Variance (ANOVA): A procedure to test statistically the equality of means of discrete factor inputs.

Attribute Data: The presence or absence of some characteristic.

Attribute Response: Information appraised in terms of whether a characteristic or property does or does not exist. It may be expressed as a non-compliance rate or proportion.

Away: The ball or golfer farthest from the hole is *away* and normally next to shoot.

Balanced scorecard (the): The balanced scorecard (Kaplan and Norton 1992) tracks business organizational functions in the areas of financial, customer, and internal business process and learning & growth. In this system, an organization's vision and strategy is also to lead to the cascading of objectives, measures, targets, and initiatives throughout the organization. This book describes issues with this system and an alternative IEE system that overcomes these shortcomings.

Benchmark: A standard in judging quality, value, or other important characteristics.

Best ball: Team competition format in which the best score of any team member is recorded on each hole.

Birdie: A hole completed in one shot under par.

Bite: Describes a ball hit with backspin, which stops or backs up on the green.

Black belts (BBs): Process improvement Lean Six Sigma and IEE practitioners who typically receive four weeks of training over four months. It is most desirable that black belts are dedicated resources; however, many organizations utilize part-time resources. During training, black belt trainees lead the execution of a project that has in-class report-outs and critiques. Between training sessions black belt trainees should receive project coaching, which is a very important for their success. They are expected to deliver high-quality report-outs to peers, champions, and executives. Upon course completion, black belts are expected to continue delivering financial beneficial projects; e.g., four to six projects per year with financial benefits of $500,000–$1,000,000. Black belts can mentor green belts.

Blind hole: Any hole where the golfer cannot see the desired target area for a shot.

Bogey: A hole completed in one shot over par.

Break: The turn of a putt to the right or left as it rolls. Also, the contour of the green that causes the putt to turn.

Bump-and-run: An approach shot to the green purposely played to hit into the face of a hill to reduce speed and then run (roll) to the hole.

Bunkers: Grass bunkers are areas on the course with severe terrain that serve as natural obstacles but are not treated as hazards. Sand or pot bunkers filled with sand are treated as hazards.

Carry: The distance a shot flies in the air. Also, to clear a hazard successfully.

Casual water: Temporary accumulation of water on the course that is not part of the course design, as from rain or sprinklers. Balls may be lifted from casual water without penalty.

Cause-and-effect diagram: Also called the fishbone or Ishikawa diagram, the C&E Diagram is a graphical brainstorming tool used to organize possible causes (KPIVs) of a symptom into categories of causes. Standard categories are considered to be materials, machine, method, personnel, measurement, and environment. These are branched as required to additional levels. It is a tool used for gathering Wisdom of the Organization.

Cause-and-effect matrix: A tool used to help quantify team consensus on relationships thought to exist between key input and key output variables. The results lead to other activities such as FMEA, multi-vari charts, ANOVA, regression analysis, and DOE.

Champions: Executive-level managers who are responsible for managing and guiding the Lean Six Sigma or IEE deployment and its projects.

Chip: Short approach shot to the green that is hit low and carries just onto the putting surface and then bounces and rolls to the hole. Also, chip and run.

CODND: Cost of doing nothing differently.

Common cause: Natural or random variation that is inherent in a process over time, affecting every outcome of the process. If a process is in-control, it has only common-cause variation and can be said to be predictable. When a process experiences common-cause variability but does not meet customer needs it can be said that the process is not capable. Process or input variable change is needed to improve this situation; i.e., this metric is creating a pull for project creation.

Confidence interval: The limits or band of a parameter that contains the true parameter value at a confidence level. The band can be single sided to describe an upper/lower limit or double sided to describe both upper and lower limits.

Continuous response: A response is said to be continuous if any value can be taken between limits. Examples include weight, distance, and voltage.

Control chart: A procedure used to track a process over time for the purpose of determining whether data are common or special cause.

Dashboard: *See* Scorecard.

Days Sales Outstanding (DSO): In general, the average number of days it takes to collect revenue after a sale has been made. In the example in the text, it is the number of days before or after the due date that a payment is received.

Dead (or Stiff): A shot right at the hole, especially if it stops close to the hole.

Divots: The piece of turf taken by a proper iron swing.

DOE (Design of Experiments): Experiment methodology in which factor levels are assessed in a fractional factorial experiment or in a full factorial experiment structure.

Dogleg: A hole where the fairway bends to the right or left. Also, the area where a fairway bends.

DMADV: These are the five IEE design project steps:

Define—Define project goals and internal/external customer deliverables

Measure—Determine customer needs and requirements

Analyze—Assess process options to address customer needs

Design—Create the product, process, or IT project to meet customer needs

Verify—Test the created product, process, or IT project for its performance and ability to satisfy customer needs

DMAIC: These are the five P-DMAIC phases:

Define—Define and scope the project.

Measure—Define smart metrics and baseline the project. Establish current, high-level metrics for the process, including the capability/performance of the process. Consider measurement systems analysis. Wisdom of the Organization assessments are a part of this phase.

Analyze—Use IEE analysis tools to find root causes. Evaluate relationships between input factors and output responses, and model processes.

Improve—Optimize processes.

Control—Institutionalize and maintain gains.

Double bogey: A hole completed in two shots over par.

DPMO (defects per million opportunities): Number of defects that, on average, occur in one million opportunities. Care should be taken to assure that all defects, including touch-ups and reworks that previously may not have been recorded, are included in this calculation. Also important is an agreed-upon standard method for counting opportunities.

Drop area: When a ball is hit into a hazard and cannot be played as it lies, it may be dropped and played from designated *drop areas*, with the appropriate penalty.

Draw: A shot that turns slightly from right to left in flight for a right-handed golfer. Also, the deliberate attempt to play a controlled shot that has *draw*. Not to be confused with a *hook*, a shot with excessive right to left movement for a right-handed golfer.

E-DMAIC (roadmap): An IEE enterprise define-measure-analyze-improve-control roadmap, which contains among other things a value chain measurement and analysis system where metric improvement needs can pull for project creation.

EIP (Enterprise Improvement Plan): A system for drilling down from business goals to specific projects, as illustrated in Figure 7.3

Fade: A shot that turns slightly from left to right in flight for a right-handed golfer. Also, the deliberate attempt to play a controlled shot that has *fade*. Not to be confused with a *slice,* a shot with excessive left to right to left movement for a right-handed golfer.

Fat: A shot that strikes the ground before impacting the ball. Often takes too much turf (too big a divot) and ends up short of the intended target.

50-foot-level metric: A low-level metric or KPIV, which can affect the response of a 30,000-foot-level metric.

5S: Procedures used to clean up and organize a work place (house-keeping): Sort, Straighten, Shine, Standardize Work, and Sustain Improvements.

FMEA (failure mode and effect analysis): A proactive method of improving reliability and minimizing failures in a product or service. It is an analytical approach to preventing problems in processes. For a process FMEA, Wisdom of the Organization is used to list what can go wrong at each step of a process that could cause potential failures or customer problems. Each item is evaluated for its importance, frequency of occurrence, and probability of detecting its occurrence. This information is used to prioritize the items that most need improving. These are then assigned a corrective action plan to reduce their risk.

Firefighting: The practice of giving much focus to fixing the problems of the day/week. The usual corrective actions taken in firefighting, such as tweaking a stable process, do not create any long-term fixes and may actually cause process degradation.

Free drop (or Relief): Slang for allowance to move the ball to an unobstructed position without penalty; e.g., from casual water or ground under repair.

Fringe: The close-cut grass surrounding the green. Also known as the apron, frog hair, or collar.

Gage R&R (repeatability and reproducibility): A tool used in Measurement Systems Analysis. It is the evaluation of measuring instruments to determine their capability to yield a precise response. It determines how much of the observed process variation is due to measurement system variation. Gage repeatability is the variation in measurements using the same measurement instrument several times by one appraiser measuring the identical characteristic on the same part. Gage reproducibility is the variation in the average of measurements made by different appraisers using the same measuring instrument when measuring the identical characteristics on the same part.

Governance, corporate: The system by which business corporations are directed and controlled. The corporate governance structure specifies the distribution of rights and responsibilities among different participants in the corporation, such as, the board, managers, shareholders and other stakeholders, and spells out the rules and procedures for making decisions on corporate affairs. By doing this, it also provides the structure through which the company objectives are set, and the means of attaining those objectives and monitoring performance. – Organization for Economic Cooperation and Development (OECD) April 1999

Green, Fast vs. Slow: Greens that are cut short or are dry and hard are typically *fast*. Putts will go farther than normal and break more on fast greens. Greens that grow longer, or are wet and soft, are often *slow*. Putts will go shorter than normal and break less on slow greens. Putts may also be referred to as *fast* or *slow*.

Grain: The direction that the grass grows, which may affect the speed and break of putts. Putts hit with the *grain* will roll farther and break less than putts against the *grain*.

Green belts (GBs): Part-time practitioners who typically receive two weeks of training over two months. Their primary focus is on projects that are in their functional area. The inference that someone becomes a green belt before a black belt should not be made. Business and personal needs/requirements should influence the decision whether someone becomes a black belt or green belt. If someone's job requires a more in-depth skill set, such as the use of Design of Experiments, then the person should be trained as a black belt. Also, at deployment initiation black belt training should be conducted first so that this additional skill set can be used when coaching others.

Ground under repair: Marked areas of the course where maintenance is being performed. Balls landing in these areas may be dropped without penalty out of the marked area but no nearer the hole.

Handicap: A system to rank golfers according to their skill levels, allowing them to engage fairly in even competition.

Hazard: Lakes, streams, ponds, creeks, ditches, bunkers, or nature areas on the golf course may be marked as *hazards*. Balls may be played from within the *hazards* or dropped out of the *hazards* with appropriate penalties.

Histogram: A graphical representation or bar graph of the sample relative frequency distribution describing the occurrence of grouped items. This graph summarizes and displays the distribution of data in an easier-to-grasp form than tables of data.

Hole Out: To complete the final stroke into the cup or hole.

Home: A shot that lands on the green is said to get *home*; e.g. get *home* in two.

Honor: The player with the lowest score on the previous hole has the *honor* on the next hole. *Honors* carry over on ties.

Individuals control chart: A control chart of individual values where between-subgroup variability affects the calculated upper and lower control limits; i.e., the width between the upper and lower control limits increases when there is more between subgroup variability. When plotted individuals chart data is within the upper and lower control limits and there are no patterns, the process is said to be stable and typically referenced as an in control process. In IEE, this common-cause state is referenced as a predictable process. Control limits are independent of specification limits or targets. Volume 3 describes the creation of this chart.

In regulation: The ideal score (par) on a hole minus two putts; i.e., the ideal number of strokes allowed to reach the green in regulation. For example, on a par four hole, getting on the green in two shots would be *in regulation.*

Integrated Enterprise (process) Excellence (IEE, I double E): A roadmap for the creation of an enterprise process system in which organizations can significantly improve both customer satisfaction and their bottom line. The techniques help manufacturing, development, and service organizations become more competitive and/or move them to new heights. IEE is a structured approach that guides organizations through the tracking and attainment of organizational goals. IEE goes well beyond traditional Lean Six Sigma and the balanced scorecard methods. IEE integrates enterprise process measures and improvement methodologies with tools such as Lean and Theory of Constraints (TOC) in a never-ending pursuit of excellence. IEE becomes an enabling framework, which integrates, improves, and aligns with other initiatives such as Total Quality Management (TQM), ISO 9000, Malcolm Baldrige Assessments, and the Shingo Prize. IEE is the organizational orchestration that moves toward the achievement goal of the three Rs of Business; i.e., everyone is doing the Right things and doing them Right at the Right time.

ISO-9000:2000: An updated version of ISO-9000. It requires that you demonstrate Improvements are being made within your processes.

ISO-9000: ISO-9000 consists of individual but related international standards on quality management and quality assurance. Developed to help companies effectively document the quality-system elements to be implemented in order to maintain an efficient quality system. It is a requirement often placed on manufacturing companies. The basic idea behind ISO-9000 methodology is that you document what you do and you do what you say. During an ISO-9000 certification process, the examining registrar will audit your company to confirm that you are following the standard. If you are, you can be certified.

Kaizen Event (or Kaizen Blitz): Kaizen is a Japanese term meaning gradual unending improvement by doing little things better and setting and achieving increasingly higher standards. A *Kaizen Event* occurs when an operation team works together to improve a specific operation. It typically involves a detailed description of the current state of the selected operation, developing the Kaizen Event plan for improvement, implementing the plan, following-up to confirm that the plan was carried out fully and correctly, and reporting to management on the event and its accomplishments.

Kanban: Pulling a product through the production process. This method of manufacturing process-flow-control only allows movement of material by pulling from a preceding process. Inventory is kept low. When quality errors are detected, less production is affected.

KPIV (key process input variable): Factors within a process correlated to an output characteristic(s) important to the internal or external customer. Optimizing and controlling these is vital to the improvement of the KPOV.

KPOV (key process output variable): Characteristic(s) of the output of a process that are important to the customer. Understanding what is important to the internal and external customer is essential to identifying KPOVs.

Lag: A conservative attempt to get close enough to (often short of) the hole so that the next putt can be made. The opposite of a bold putt that may go far past the hole and leave a difficult second putt.

Lay Up: A strategic shot played short of the green or hazard intended to leave a safe play on the next shot.

Lean: An approach to producing products or services focusing on reducing total cycle time and costs by reducing waste, improving flow, and striving for excellence.

Left Edge, Right Edge: The left or right edges of the hole or green may be used as aiming targets when allowing for the break or the wind.

Level Five System: Collins (2001) describes in *Good to Great* a level five leader as someone who is not only great when he is leading an organization but the organization remains great after the person is no longer affiliated with the organization. I describe the level-five-leader-created legacy as being a *Level Five System.*

Lie: The position of the ball in the grass (good, buried, tight, fluffy) or relative to the terrain (level, uphill, downhill, side hill). Also, the angle of the club head to the shaft (upright, standard, or flat).

Long irons: Typically 1, 2, 3, and 4 irons.

Master black belts (MBBs): Black belts who have undertaken two weeks of advanced training and have a proven track record delivering results through various projects and project teams. They should be a dedicated resource to the deployment. Before they train, master black belts need to be certified in the material that they are to deliver. Their responsibilities include coaching black belts, monitoring team progress, and assisting teams when needed.

Matches: Games, league competitions, or wagers.

Match play: Competition format in which the winner is determined by the number of holes won rather than by total strokes (stroke play).

MBA: Master of Business Administration.

Mean: Sum of all responses divided by the sample size.

Measurement Systems Analysis: Analysis of the complete process of obtaining measurements. This includes the collection of equipment, operations, procedures, software, and personnel that affects the assignment of a number to a measurement characteristic. Includes, but is not limited to, Gage R&R.

Median: For a sample, the number that is in the middle when all observations are ranked in magnitude. For a population, the value at which the cumulative distribution function is 0.5.

Muda: A Japanese term indicating efforts that do not add value (waste). Some categories of *muda* are defects, over production or excess inventory, idle time, and poor layout.

Multi-vari chart: A chart that displays the variance within units, between units, between samples, and between lots. It is useful in detecting variation sources within a process.

Net: Score on a hole or round after the handicap has been deducted from the gross score.

Obstructions: Man-made objects such as cart paths, benches, etc. that are not part of the course design. Typically, a free drop may be given when a golfer's ball, stance, or shot path is impeded by an obstruction.

Out: The ball or player farthest from the hole. Also away.

Out-of-bounds (OB): A ball that has gone beyond the designated area of play for the hole (normally marked by white stakes). When a ball is hit OB in tournament competition, the golfer must play another ball from the original spot with a one-stroke penalty. In recreational play, it is customary for the new ball to be dropped just inside the fairway closest to where the ball left the fairway with a one-stroke penalty.

Pairing: Players scheduled to play together as competitors or partners.

Par: The regulation number of strokes set for a hole played perfectly, determined by yardage and hole design.

Passive analysis: Data collected and analyzed as the process is currently performing to determine potential KPIVs. Process alterations are not assessed.

P-DMAIC (Roadmap): An IEE project define-measure-analyze-improve-control roadmap for improvement project execution, which contains a true integration of Six Sigma and Lean tools.

PGA Tour: The series of Professional Golfers Association Tournaments.

Pick up: Picking up a ball before the hole is completed. In match play or recreational play, a golfer may tell an opponent to "pick it up." Not applicable in stroke play competition.

Pin placement: Hole location on the green. A pin placed in the middle of a large green may be called an *easy* pin placement, while one hidden close behind a bunker is called a *tough* or *sucker* pin placement.

Pitch: A short, high approach shot into the green, which lands softly and doesn't roll too far.

Pitch In or Chip In: A pitch or chip shot that goes directly into the hole from off the green.

P-DMAIC: *See* DMAIC.

Poka-Yoke: A Japanese term indicating a mechanism that either prevents a mistake from occurring or makes a mistake obvious at a glance.

PPM (parts per million): An attribute measurement of defect rate, expressed in defects found divided by one million. Percent defects were once the standard. Note that a percentage-unit-improvement in parts-per-million (ppm) defect rate does not equate to the same percentage improvement in the sigma quality level.

PPMO (parts per million opportunities): A defect-per-unit calculation giving additional insight into a process by including the number of opportunities for failure. When this is done, the metric is DPMO. Care must be taken in estimating the number of opportunities for defects in a process.

Predictable process: A stable, controlled process where variation in outputs is only caused by natural or random variation in the inputs or in the process itself.

Probability plot: Data are plotted on a selected probability paper coordinate system to determine if a particular distribution is appropriate (i.e., the data plot as a straight line) and to make statements about percentiles of the population. The plot can be used to make prediction statements about stable processes. Volume 3 describes the creation of this plot.

Process capability/performance metric: IEE uses the term process capability/performance metric to describe a process's predictive output in terms that everyone can understand. The process to determine this metric is: 1. An infrequent subgrouping and sampling plan is determined so that the typical variability from process input factors occurs between subgroups, e.g., subgroup by day, week, or month. 2. The process is analyzed for predictability using control charts. 3. For the region of predictability, the non-compliant proportion or parts per million (ppm) are estimated and reported. If there are no specifications, the estimated median response and 80% frequency of occurrence are reported.

Process Capability/Performance: A measure of the ability of a process to produce output that is within the customer requirement or specification.

Pull: A Lean term that results in an activity when a customer or down-stream process step requests the activity. A homebuilder that builds houses only when an agreement is reached on the sale of the house is using a pull system. *See* Push.

Pull for project creation: This term is derived from the Lean term, pull. An IEE deployment objective is that performance metric ownership is assigned through the business value chain, where metric tracking is at the 30,000-foot-level. In the E-DMAIC process, the enterprise is analyzed as a whole to determine what performance metrics need improvement and by how much so that whole-organizational goals can be met. These metric improvement needs would then create a pull for project creation. *See* Push for project creation.

Push: A Lean term that results in an activity that a customer or down-stream process step has not specifically requested. This activity can create excessive waste and/or inventory. A home-builder that builds houses on the speculation of sale is using a push system. If the house does not sell promptly upon completion, the homebuilder has created excess inventory for his company, which can be very costly. *See* Pull.

Push for project creation: This term is derived from the Lean term, push. Lean Six Sigma deployments are to create and execute projects that are to be beneficial to the business. However, when assessing the typical Lean Six Sigma project selection process we note that either a deployment steering committee or some level of management selects projects from a list that they and others think are important. For this type of deployment, for example, there is often a scurry to determine a project to work on during training. I refer this system as a push for project creation; i.e., people are hunting for projects because they need to get certified or whatever. With this deployment system, there can be initial successes since agree-to low hanging fruit projects can often be readily identified and provide significant benefits; however, it has been my experience that this system of project determination is not typically long lasting. After some period of time, people have a hard time defining and/or agreeing to what projects should be undertaken. In addition, this project creation system does not typically look at the system as a whole when defining projects to undertake. This system of project selection can lead to sub-optimization, which could be detrimental enterprise as a whole. Finally, this Lean Six Sigma deployment system typically creates a separate function entity that manages the deployment, which is separate from operational scorecards and functional units. In time, people in these functions can be very visible on the corporate radar screen when downsizing forces occur or their in a change in executive management, even thought the function has been claiming much past success. *See* Pull for project creation.

Putt out: To putt the ball into the hole. Also, to continue putting after the first putt, even if the golfer is not *away.*

Putting line: The line a putt follows to the hole on the green, determined by the slope and contour of the green.

Reading a putt: The act of estimating the speed and line of a putt before putting.

Regression or Regression analysis: A defined process for quantifying and modeling the response (KPOV) of a process relative to its input variables. It estimates the relationship between KPIVs and the KPOV of a process and produces a mathematical model of that relationship. Its use can lead to a better understanding of the critical factors controlling the quality of the process output.

Relief: Shots that come to rest in an obstruction or *ground under repair* may be entitled to *relief. See* Free drop.

Robust process: A process is considered robust when its output variability is not sensitive to the normal variation from its input variables. For example, a manufacturing process step is robust to different operators who normally execute the operation step.

Rough: The area of the course off the fairway, not in a hazard, where the grass is often allowed to grow taller.

Sand traps: Hazards filled with sand. They are often positioned close to landing areas either near the fairway or the green.

Satellite-level: Used to describe a high level IEE business metric that has infrequent subgrouping/sampling so that short-term variations, which might be caused by the variation key process input variables, will result in control charts that view these perturbations as common-cause variations. This metric has no calendar boundaries and the latest region of stability can be used to provide a predictive statement of the future.

Scorecard: A scorecard is to help manage an organization's performance through the optimization and alignment of organizational units, business processes, and individuals. A scorecard can also provide goals and targets, which is to help individuals understand their organizational contribution. Scorecards span the operational, tactical and strategic business aspects and decisions. A dashboard is to display information so that an enterprise can be run effectively. A dashboard is to organize and present information in a format that is easy to read and interpret. In this series of book volumes, I make reference to the IEE performance measurement as either a scorecard or scorecard/dashboard.

Scoring: The grooves on the face of the club, especially irons. It may also refer to the act of shooting low scores.

Scramble: A team competition in which all team members hit their shot and choose the best ball position from which to shoot their next round of shots. This is repeated until the team holes out.

Scratch: A term used to describe a golfer who shoots par or has a zero handicap.

Short game: Approach shots and putts. The part of the game that is typically inside approximately 100 yards from the hole.

Short hitter: A player who doesn't hit the ball far or hits shortest off the tee.

Short irons: Typically the 7, 8, and 9 irons, and the pitching, gap, sand, and lob wedges.

Sigma quality level: A metric calculated by some to describe the capability of a process relative to its specification. A six sigma quality level is said to have a 3.4 ppm rate.

Skin: A game in which an amount is bet on each hole; e.g., dime skins. The lowest score on a hole wins, but if two players tie, all tie, and the pot rolls over until someone records a skin.

SMART goals: Not everyone uses the same letter descriptors for SMART. My preferred descriptors are italicized in the following list: S—*specific*, significant, stretching; M—*measurable*, meaningful, motivational; A—agreed upon, attainable, achievable, acceptable, action-oriented, *actionable*; R—realistic, *relevant*, reasonable, rewarding, results-oriented; T—*time-based*, timely, tangible, trackable.

Special cause: Variation in a process from a cause that is not an inherent part of that process. That is, it's not a common cause.

Standard deviation: A mathematical quantity that quantifies the variability of a response.

Starter: Course employee in charge of tee times.

The balanced scorecard: *See* Balanced scorecard (the).

Thin: A shot that catches the ball with the sole of the club. *Thin* shots may damage the ball or produce uncontrolled low shots.

Three Rs of business: Everyone doing the Right things and doing them Right at the Right time.

Tee box: The tee area at the start of each hole.

Tees, Red, White, or Blue: Within a tee box, red tees indicate positions from which ladies tee off. White tees are commonly used by average players. Blue tees may be championship tees. Other colors may be used, depending on local course convention. Tee colors indicate the starting position for players who have different skill levels.

Theory of Constraints (TOC): Goldratt (1992) describes in his book, *The Goal*, a model that challenges many traditional accounting and business practices. He makes the case that we often do not know what our true business goal is. One goal every business shares is the need to be profitable. A particular business will have other goals as well. These goals must be well thought out, clearly stated, and communicated to everyone in the organization. Goldratt's procedures focus on three metrics: throughput (the rate at which the system produces income), inventory (all the money the system invests in things to sell as well as all money tied up in the system), and operating expense (money spent turning inventory into throughput). The constraints that prevent achieving our goal(s) are primarily system restraints. Therefore, we must determine what to change, what to change to, and how to cause change. Goldratt describes five sequential steps to remove constraints and progress toward a goal:

1. Identify the system Constraint
2. Decide how to exploit the Constraint
3. Subordinate everything else
4. Elevate the Constraint
5. Go back to step one

30,000-foot-level metric: A high-level, big-picture, long-term measure of an operational or project process metric used in an IEE strategy. A 30,000-foot-level control chart would be used to separate common-cause variation in a process from special cause. This metric can improve the understanding of process variation and can redirect firefighting activities (i.e., reacting to all unsatisfactory output as if it were a special cause) to fire-prevention activities (i.e., using a team to systematically improve the process through a P-DMAIC strategy). This measurement can be used to baseline a process before beginning a project and then to track the project's progress.

Total Quality Management (TQM): There are many definitions of this term. It is an approach to quality that uses management practices and quality tools to improve quality continuously to customers. It is believed that the term was initially coined in 1985 by the Naval Air Systems Command to describe its Japanese-style management approach to quality improvement. The methods used are gleaned from the teachings of quality leaders such as Deming, Juran, Feigenbaum, Crosby, and Ishikawa. Feigenbaum originated the concept of total quality control in his book *Total Quality Control*, published in 1951.

Turn: The start of the back nine is often called the *turn*. Historically, older links courses used to go out in one direction for nine holes and make the turn before coming back to the clubhouse.

Two-putt: The standard allowance for putting when computing par. Two putts are considered to complete the hole once the ball reaches the green.

Unplayable lie: A ball in a position that cannot be played, as determined by the player. Standard rules for *relief* with penalty apply.

Value chain: Describes in flowchart fashion both primary and support organizational activities and their accompanying 30,000-foot-level or satellite-level metrics. Example primary activity flow is develop product—market product—sell product—produce product—invoice/collect payments—report satellite-level metrics. Example support activities include IT, finance, HR, labor relations, safety & environment, and legal.

References

Breyfogle, F. W., J. M. Cupello, and B. Meadows. 2001. *Managing Six Sigma: A Practical Guide to Understanding, Assessing, and Implementing the Strategy that Yields Bottom-Line Success.* New York: Wiley.

Breyfogle, F. W., D. Enck, P. Flories, and T. Pearson. 2001. *Wisdom on the Green: Smarter Six Sigma Business Solutions.* Austin, TX: Smarter Solutions, Inc.

Breyfogle, F. W. 2003. *Implementing Six Sigma: Smarter Solutions® Using Statistical Methods.* 2d ed. Hoboken, NJ: Wiley.

Breyfogle, F. W. 2004. "Starting a Six Sigma Initiative," *ISixSigma, Ask the Expert,* http://www.isixsigma.com/library/content/ask-05.asp.

Breyfogle, F. W. 2005. 21 common problems (and what to do about them). *Six Sigma Forum Magazine* 4 (August): 35-7.

Breyfogle, F. W. 2008a. *Integrated Enterprise Excellence, Volume I— The Basics: Golfing Buddies Go Beyond Lean Six Sigma and the Balanced Scorecard.* Austin, TX: Bridgeway Books.

Breyfogle, F. W. 2008b. *Integrated Enterprise Excellence, Volume II— Business Deployment: A Leaders' Guide for Going Beyond Lean Six Sigma and the Balanced Scorecard,.* Austin, TX: Bridgeway Books.

Breyfogle, F. W. 2008c. *Integrated Enterprise Excellence, Volume III— Improvement Project Execution: A Management and Black Belt Guide for Going Beyond Lean Six Sigma and the Balanced Scorecard.* Austin, TX: Bridgeway Books.

Breyfogle, F. W. 2008d. *The Integrated Enterprise Excellence System: An Enhanced, Unified Approach to Balanced Scorecards, Strategic Planning, and Business Improvement.* Austin, TX: Bridgeway Books.

Collins, J. 2001. *Good to Great: Why Some Companies Make the Leap... and Others Don't.* New York: HarperCollins Publishers Inc.

Goldratt, E. M. 1992. *The Goal.* 2d ed. New York: North River Press.

Kaplan, R. S. and D. P. Norton. 1992. The balanced scorecard – measures that drive performance. *Harvard Business Review,* Jan.–Feb.

Kelly, Jason (2006), *CEO firings at a record pace so far this year: Leaders are getting pushed aside as boards, wary of Enron-type problems, become more vigilant,* Bloomberg News, Austin American Statesman, October 1, 2006.

Penick, H., with B. Shrake. 1992. *Harvey Penick's Little Red Book,* New York: Simon & Schuster.

Senge, P. M. 1990. *The Fifth Discipline: The Art and Practice of the Learning Organization.* New York: Doubleday/Current.

Index